Air and Rain Penetration of Buildings

Paul Marsh

THE CONSTRUCTION PRESS LTD

LANCASTER   LONDON   NEW YORK

7 8.95

Air
and Rain
Penetration
of
Buildings

A subsidiary company of Longman Group Ltd., London
Associated companies, branches and representatives
throughout the world.

Published in the United States of America by
Longman Inc. New York.

First published 1977

ISBN 0 904406 31 8

Printed by: A. Wheaton and Company, Exeter, England.

ACKNOWLEDGEMENTS

The author acknowledges the help and advice given by the following during the preparation of this book:

S. Armsdon	The Aluminium Window Association
P. Dawe	British Standards Institution
H.W. Harrison	Building Research Establishment
R. Howorth	Miles Redfern Construction Services
N.P. Skinner	Building Research Establishment, Princes Risborough Laboratory

The following manufacturers have also assisted by generous provision of information:

Adshead Ratcliffe & Co. Ltd.	Mastics, glazing compounds
Colbrand Ltd.	Gaskets, membranes
Dow Chemical Co. Ltd.	Roof insulation
Evode Waterproofing Systems Ltd.	Sealants, membranes, remedial coatings
Expandite Ltd.	Sealants, expansion jointing, remedial coatings
Kelseal Ltd.	Sealants, glazing compounds
Marley Ltd.	Roofing membranes, plastic siding
Miles Redfern Construction Services	Gaskets
Thomas Ness Ltd.	Membranes, remedial coatings
Ruberoid Co. Ltd.	Bitumen felt, d.p. membranes, corrugated vinyl
Sealmaster Ltd.	Weather and draught seals
Tesa Tapes Ltd.	Self-adhesive foam strip
Tremco Ltd.	Membranes, sealants, glazing compounds
Unibond Ltd.	Membranes, bonding agents

Preface

"The joint is almost universally the weakest link in any combination of parts..."

K.H. Taylor

Since Man began to emulate the animal kingdom's instinctive builders and started to construct his own shelters rather than make use of what Nature had provided for him, his main concern has been the exclusion of the least congenial characteristics of the weather in whichever part of the world he was building. In creating an acceptable internal environment for himself and his family, he has needed to produce dry conditions and a temperature range within tolerable limits. In order to do this he has had to exclude completely snow and rain (airborne moisture), and to restrict or maintain the degree of air penetration as near as possible to optimal levels, depending on the temperature. In addition he has had to construct his walls and roofs so as to keep the heat either in, or out — even to control the amount of sun penetration in some parts of the world.

Today, to the list of climatic controls that the building shell has to achieve can be added the control of an undesirable airborne pollutant created by Man himself — external noise. Assuming structural soundness, the performance requirements of a building shell could be stated thus:

the exclusion of draughts and airborne water

the provision of adequate levels of thermal insulation

the control of solar temperature gain

the attenuation of external noise

Of these four performance requirements the most important (and the one with which this book is concerned) is the first. The other requirements are reserved for examination in a later book. The exclusion of airborne moisture is no less of a problem today than ever it was, in spite of our present alleged sophistication. To some extent the problem becomes more critical as our sophistication increases.

The more we rely on light, thin, easy-to-assemble walling components rather than on heavy, thick, slow-to-construct walls of brick or stone, the more the penetration of water through the walling material needs careful thought. The mere thickness of the wall no longer overcomes the natural absorbency of the walling material, or the inefficiency of the joints. Both material absorbency and joint efficiency need scientific assessment if water penetration is to be avoided. The higher we build, the more rigorous are the conditions our building envelopes have to withstand. As exposure increases with height, so the force with which water is hurled at the building surface increases, as does the quantity of water flowing down the lower levels of the walls.

New building techniques create new problems of water exclusion. Two identically sized buildings, one of load-bearing brickwork and one clad in pre-cast concrete panels, present two completely different sets of problems. As the use of prefabricated external elements increases, so the demand will grow for greater skill in the design of joints. Most designers can recall examples of failure — such as new buildings assailed with mastic guns in order to try to hold at bay the ever-inquisitive advances of water — all indicating a failure to appreciate, or inability to solve, the problem at the design stage.

This ready-reference book will assist the designer both to appreciate and to solve his present-day problems of airborne water and air penetration. As the problem of water penetration is universal and is wholly associated with climatic and meteorological factors, it has been decided to take a deliberately broad view, establishing principles of design which will apply to all areas of the world (some of which have a greater water penetration problem than has the United Kingdom). Thus we start with an examination of the meteorological factors which give rise to the problem and the methods whereby expected conditions can be simulated in tests to establish the viability of various design solutions. We then examine the two main surfaces of a building — walls and roofs — which are primarily involved in the exclusion of airborne water, and set down for various forms of construction the types of detail most likely to be successful. Finally a study is made of various proprietary materials and systems designed and marketed specifically to overcome the water-exclusion problem. Both UK and overseas design standards are referred to wherever these are relevant.

Contents

1 The Physical Background

All buildings, whatever shortcomings they may have, are required to possess two fundamental characteristics. They should be structurally sound and they should exclude moisture. The latter characteristic can be sub-divided in accordance with the type of moisture to be excluded – airborne (rain or snow), or groundborne. Of these two categories the former presents the greater problem, largely due to a poverty, until recently, of information on how to make watertight the non-traditional assemblies of pre-formed components that make up many of today's buildings. The difficulty has been aggravated by a less than adequate understanding of precisely why building assemblies leak. This is the problem which we now examine.

The exclusion of moisture (that is, the weather-proofness of a building) is one of a long list of performance characteristics which a building shell needs to possess in varying degrees in order to achieve an internal environment within tolerable limits for the occupants of the building. Other character-istics spring readily to mind – the insulation of the shell of a building to maintain satisfactory internal heat levels, the control of the amount of external light penetrating the shell of the building, the avoidance of internal moisture build-up (condensation), the exclusion of noise, the achievement of acceptable levels of natural ventilation, and so on. Given structural soundness, of all the additional characteristics that could be listed it is in one more than in any other where failure renders the building totally unsatisfac-tory – the exclusion of moisture. Also, failure in this aspect – due probably to human failure to appreciate and assess the problem at the design stage – can prove exceedingly expensive and difficult, if not impossible, to rectify in the completed building. Next to structural soundness, therefore, weather-proofness is without doubt the most important characteristic a building needs to possess.

The penetration of a building's shell by airborne moisture is associated with two climatic factors – rain and wind. Without wind the rain would fall vertically, barely wetting a building's walls; without wind there would be little or no air pressure difference between the inside and outside of a build-ing, so draughts which help to force moisture inside the building shell would not exist. Thus air and rain penetration cannot be dissociated; they are two parts of the same problem. It must be clearly understood that air penetration in this context is unconnected with natural ventilation, which is another factor on our list of performance characteristics; but failure to control and keep within tolerable limits casual air intrusion will affect not only ventila-tion, but also heat control.

In a survey on the weathertightness of buildings carried out in 1960 by the Building Research Establishment, the scale of the problem in relation to buildings with light facades (i.e. those composed of pre-formed elements — curtain walling, wall panels, etc.) was highlighted. Twenty per cent of the buildings examined were found to be leaking to some extent. Quite simply, the principles of building technology had been changing since the early decades of this century and, as is often the case, necessary adjustments had not been made in the supporting techniques. Not only were buildings frequently being constructed to greater heights than before, but they were being assembled from a series of thin, pre-formed parts, thus placing considerably greater importance on the weathertightness of their joints. Whereas in traditional construction mere thickness of walls and a pitched roof had often maintained dry conditions inside, changes in the economic situation had led to the adoption of different building techniques with different problems.

Means of moisture entry

The penetration of a building shell by airborne moisture can result from:—

a) the absorbency of the material of which the shell is made

b) a failure of the joints between elements of the shell made of the same material, or

c) a failure of the joints between elements of the shell made of differing materials (i.e. walling and window frame).

All three forms of breakdown are associated with the degree of exposure to which the building is subjected — in other words, the velocity and duration of the wind that is driving the rain and the direction of such wind relative to the building surface.

It is, therefore, important to consider first the climatic factors that affect the rain penetration of buildings, and then the way rainwater flows over a building's surfaces.

CLIMATIC AND METEOROLOGICAL FACTORS

In and around London, on average, it is raining for 5% of the time. On the western coast of England and Wales this figure increases to 8%, and to over 10% in hilly districts. In large areas of northwest Scotland rain can be expected for 15% of the time. In spite of our belief in the U.K. that we have an excessively wet climate, there are many places in the world where annual rainfall not only exceeds ours, but also occurs within considerably shorter periods. We do, however, experience a wide range of rainfall. The wettest place in Britain on record is Sprinkling Tarn in Cumbria, where 6528 mm of rain fell in 1954. London, on the other hand, has an average rainfall of 580 mm. Generally, rainfall in Britain increases with height and distance from the east coast. Many areas experience less than 650 mm of rain per year — the coastal areas of Essex, Suffolk, Norfolk and Lincolnshire, the lowland area running south from the Wash and the area in the rain shadow to the east of the Pennines. Only very few areas experience over 2500 mm of rain per year and these are restricted to high ground in Snowdonia, the Lake District and the northwest Highlands. It is interesting to compare the rainfall figures recorded in London (Kew) with some from more extreme climates.

Table 1/1 Comparative rainfall (in millimetres)

Rainfall (mm)	London (UK)	Bombay (India)	Monrovia (Liberia)	Cairo (Egypt)	Suva (Fiji)	Lagos (Nigeria)
Monthly average						
Maximum	64	617	995	5	368	460
Minimum	36	less than 3	31	less than 3	124	–
Annual average	580	1808	5140	28	2974	1836
Max. in 24 hrs.	56	549	363	38	673	226

All the figures in Table 1/1 (with the exception of those for Cairo), in contrast to the more consistent figures from London, show large extremes of rainfall. Cairo, it will be seen, has consistently little rain. Several interesting conclusions can be made. Bombay acquires its 1808 mm average annual total rainfall with the widest range of average monthly figures. Its minimum monthly figure is little more than 0.4% of its maximum monthly figure, indicating a great intensity of rain during the monsoon season — a fact borne out by the enormous maximum daily figure. Compared with Bombay, Lagos with a similar annual rainfall has a more even spread of rain throughout the year. The outstanding annual rainfall, that of Monrovia, also shows an uneven spread over the months, the minimum figure being only 3% of the maximum. It is interesting to note that Monrovia's annual *average* rainfall does not reach the phenomenal *maximum* figure achieved by Sprinkling Tarn in 1954.

It is the association of wind speed with rainfall that gives many places in the U.K. conditions of critical exposure that are only rarely exceeded in the rest of Europe, North America and many other places in the world. Figure 1/1 shows the British Isles with contours indicating the maximum 3 second gust speeds in metres per second which are unlikely to be exceeded in 50 years at a height of 10 m above the ground in open country. This map forms the basis of the British Standards Institution method of assessing the performance of windows (see also Chapters 2 and 3). Figure 1/2 is a further map, giving in simplified form the mean hourly wind speeds in m/s at 10 m above ground level. This is used by the Interdepartmental Construction Development Group (of the Departments of Education and Science, Environment, Health and Social Security and the Scottish Development Department) — ICDG — as a basis for the assessment of the leakage performance of windows in different exposure areas. Wind speed has become the usual basis for assessment of performance of windows and doors, to establish not only air leakage (from the pressure difference) but also water leakage. Performance grades are then established against exposure areas on whichever map is used. The Agrément Board employs its own exposure map which is a statistical combination of maximum 3 second gust data and mean wind speed (see Figure 2/4).

The performance of walls and their permeability is generally set against exposure gradings derived from the driving-rain index. Although the U.K. weather pattern is used here to establish principles of exposure, the methods are universal and can be applied to other geographical areas — given the availability of meteorological data for those areas.

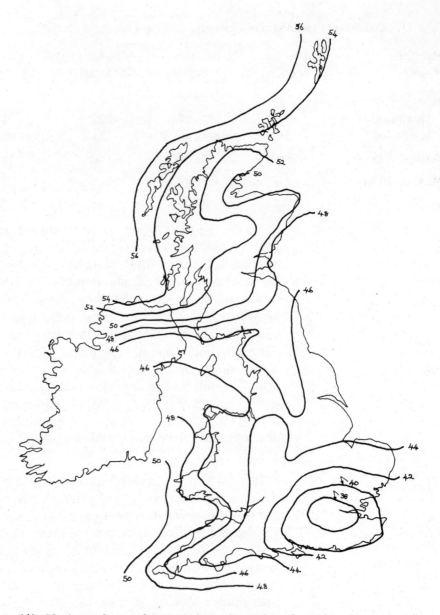

Figure 1/1   Maximum 3 second gust wind speed map (in m/s at 10 m above ground) based on Meteorological Office information.

Driving-rain index

The likelihood of rain penetration, particularly through vertical surfaces, is based not solely on the quantity of rainfall, but on a combination of this and wind speed. In the absence of wind, rain would fall vertically and the slightest projection on a wall would be sufficient to protect the entire wall from wetting. This condition of complete calm is, to say the least, unusual.

The angle at which rain strikes a wall depends on a combination of wind speed and raindrop size. Clearly the larger the raindrops, the greater their tendency to fall vertically and the greater the wind speed necessary to induce an angle of deviation from the vertical.

It can be appreciated that wind speed plays an important part in the question of rain penetration, particularly through permeable wall surfaces, and it is not surprising that a direct relationship exists between the amount of rain which falls on a wall face and the degree of exposure of the site. The Building Research Establishment (BRE) have carried out an assessment of driving rain which is explained in their Digest 127. During a period of three

14

Figure 1/2 Simplified mean hourly wind speed map (in m/s at 10 m above ground) based on Meteorological Office information.

winter months a west facing driving-rain gauge at Garston, Hertfordshire, collected 20 litres/m² in the nine worst storms of the period. A similarly positioned gauge on the outskirts of a town in South Wales collected 304 litres/m² during the nine worst storms in that area during a similar period. A relatively short distance between reading points, however, can produce significantly different results; and a gauge placed in a park in the same Welsh town on occasions collected only 1/15th of the rain collected on the outskirts of the town, although there was a difference in elevation of only 90 m.

Maps of average wind speeds indicate that in the U.K. highest speeds occur near the coasts (especially the western coasts) while inland areas are relatively sheltered, except for local increases in wind speeds in hilly areas. Clearly, driven rain must be directly related to this type of pattern. The BRE has discovered that the amount of rain driven on to a wall is directly proportional to the product of the rainfall on the ground and the wind speed during rain. As wind speeds during periods of rain are not usually

Figure 1/3 Simplified driving-rain index map (in m²/s).

separately recorded, the annual average wind speed is used in the establishment of a driving-rain index. This has been found to be sufficiently accurate, as there is an almost constant relationship between annual average
wind speeds and average wind speeds during rain.

The calculation of the driving-rain index (and therefore the exposure
grading) for a particular area can be made by the following formula:

$$\frac{\text{Annual rainfall (mm) x average wind speed (m/s)}}{1000}$$

This index is expressed in m²/s. It does not give an absolute value,
although an index of lm²/s approximately corresponds to 200 litres/m²
catch of driving rain on a vertical surface. The map in Figure 1/3 shows contours of driving-rain indices. This map is based on a revised one produced by
the BRE, the revision having more accurate and more frequent contours
than the earlier version as a result of using a greater quantity of meteorological data than had previously been available. It is interesting to compare the

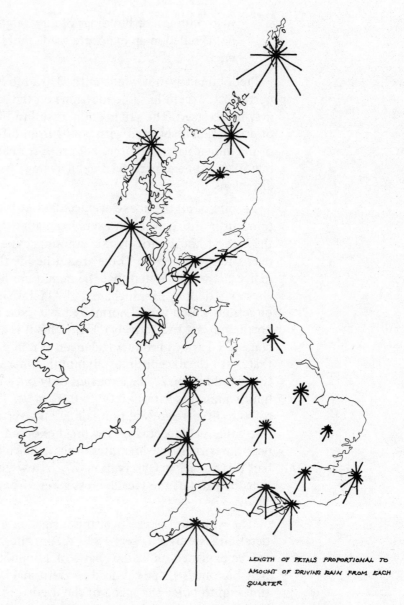

LENGTH OF PETALS PROPORTIONAL TO AMOUNT OF DRIVING RAIN FROM EACH QUARTER

Figure 1/4   Driving-rain rose map (derived from BRE Digest No 127).

driving-rain index map with the average rainfall and average wind speed maps. Driving-rain index contours indicate the total amount of rain that would be driven in one year on to a vertical surface facing the wind.

Exposure grades

Three exposure gradings are indicated on the map. Up to a driving-rain index of 3 m² /s the exposure is considered *sheltered*; from 3 to 7 m² /s *moderate*, and from 7 to 20 m² /s *severe*. These gradings may need adjustment to take into account local conditions, such as closeness to the coast, the elevation of the site or the height of the building. The following guide lines should be adhered to:—

a) *Sheltered* grading should not include areas lying within 8 km of the sea or large estuary. Such areas should be regraded *moderate*.

b) *Moderate* grading should not include areas having an index of 5 m²/s or more which are within 8 km of the sea or large estuaries. Such areas should be regraded *severe*.

c) In *sheltered* or *moderate* areas, high buildings standing above their surroundings, or buildings of any height on hill tops or slopes should be regraded in an exposure grade more severe than indicated on the map.

Predominantly wet winds in the U.K. blow from the south, west or northwest, except in some locations on the east coast where the directions may be reversed. The driving-rain 'roses' in Figure 1/4 illustrate the amounts of driven rain associated with winds from different directions. The lengths of the individual 'petal' lines are proportionate to the amount of driving rain likely to be experienced in an average year from those particular directions.

In spite of all the above *average* data, it is possible for intense driving rain to occur in short, sharp showers from almost any direction. Table 1/2 shows the highest hourly driving-rain amounts experienced by 23 weather stations over a ten year period. These are set beside the annual mean driving-rain indices. It will be noted that the maximum hourly figures for Cardiff, Manchester, London, Birmingham and Aldergrove were associated with wind directions which would normally have given little rain (north, east, east, north and east respectively). From this it is clear that no quarter can be considered as not producing danger of rain penetration. The table indicates that, with the exception of Plymouth, where an hourly rainfall is recorded that would normally be expected only once in 100 years, the range of hourly amounts is from 0.09 to 0.21 m^2/s. This is approximately equivalent to 20 to 40 litres/m^2 of rain falling on a vertical surface in one hour. This rate could be expected on the most exposed parts of the building shell — near the corners — while rates over the facade as a whole could be about half this quantity. Observation of window failure on long elevations suggests that the parts of the facade most severely exposed are as shown on Figure 1/5.

The way wind passes over the surface of a building needs careful consideration. The BRE Digest 119 explains the variations in wind pressure that can be expected on various parts of a building shell. The turbulences caused by a building's shape can lead to abnormal build-up of wind speeds, sometimes up to twice the speed of the undisturbed flow. Such points of turbulence occur at corners of walls, edges of roofs, and at cornices, with consequent local increases of the driving-rain index. The designer needs to be aware of these areas of potential danger and should remove points of weakness in his weathertight shell as far as possible from them. It would be foolish, for instance, to have more joints near the corners of a building than are necessary. In fact it is advisable to keep all wall joints at least 200 mm from corners whenever this is possible.

Another climatic factor which can lead to rain penetration is that associated with retained water in the building shell. Porous materials (and most building materials are to some extent porous) absorb some of the rain that falls on them. This is later removed by natural evaporation; such evaporation is effected by solar radiation, wind and low atmospheric humidity. The nature of the material composing the building shell will play a substantial part in the speed of evaporation. Nevertheless, in comparative examples of like materials in different climatic areas, it is evident that the wetter the area, the longer the material retains its moisture. As a result we should expect building shells to be generally wetter for longer periods on the western coasts than in eastern inland areas. This effect can intensify (albeit only slightly) the risk of rain penetration in areas with a high driving-rain index.

The way in which rain-water runs off the surfaces of a building and the extent to which this flow can be controlled by detailing are important design factors which will substantially affect the weathertightness of a building. They will be dealt with in detail in the following chapters. Other climatic effects — dimensional changes of building elements due to climatic variations, and the effect of ultra-violet radiation on joint seals — will also be considered later.

Table 1/2   Highest hourly driving rain amounts (derived from BRE Digest 127)

Place	Altitude (metres)	Annual mean DRI (m^2/s)	Maximum hourly driving-rain index			
			Amount (m^2/s)	% of annual mean DRI	Wind direction (degrees)	Month
Lerwick	82	10.60	0.117	1.1	180	December
Wick	36	6.37	0.169	2.6	030	August
Stornoway	3	9.34	0.104	1.1	240	August
Kinloss	5	2.99	0.099	3.3	030	June
Edinburgh (Turnhouse)	35	3.68	0.096	2.6	060	September
Tiree	9	10.25	0.181	1.8	150	September
Glasgow (Renfrew)	5	5.51	0.205	3.7	060	June
Prestwick	16	5.69	0.125	2.2	030	August
Dishforth-Leeming	32	3.39	0.211	6.2	240	June
Waddington	68	3.46	0.107	3.1	120	August
Mildenhall	5	2.33	0.104	4.5	270	August
Birmingham (Elmdon)	97	3.88	0.094	2.4	360	November
London (Heathrow)	25	3.37	0.140	4.1	090	July
Kew	5	2.75	0.078	2.8	030	July
Manston	44	4.45	0.086	1.9	240	January
Thorney Island	3	4.42	0.110	2.5	210	September
Boscombe Down	126	4.82	0.147	3.1	300	August
Manchester (Ringway)	76	4.87	0.167	3.4	090	September
Holyhead (Valley)	10	8.18	0.178	2.2	210	September
Aberporth	133	7.67	0.146	1.9	240	December
Cardiff (Rhoose)	62	5.82	0.199	3.4	360	August
Plymouth (Mt. Batten)	27	9.08	0.404	4.5	090	July
Aldergrove	69	5.74	0.112	2.0	090	December

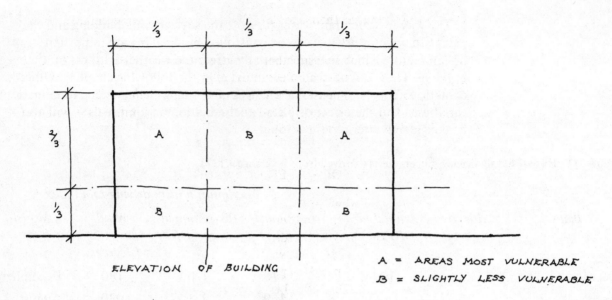

ELEVATION OF BUILDING

A = AREAS MOST VULNERABLE
B = SLIGHTLY LESS VULNERABLE

Figure 1/5 Areas of greatest incidence of window failure.

Application of meteorological data

The application of meteorological data is of necessity somewhat imprecise and does not quantify the problem in absolute terms. However, using a comparative basis of assessment, it is possible to arrive at fairly safe guidelines to follow.

Firstly, it is possible to establish an accurate assessment of the severity of exposure of a particular site using the driving-rain index map. This assessment must then be modified, taking into account any special local conditions that may apply — is the site protected by a hill or belt of woodland on the windward side? Or is it on a windward slope or on top of even a slight hill?

Having established the site exposure, a comparison should then be made of similar buildings in similar exposure zones, and their success or failure assessed. From this the designer can draw fairly accurate conclusions as to the types of problem with which he has to contend and can take steps to solve them on the drawing board (rather than at a later date as a remedial measure on site).

In making the comparative study, care should be taken to compare buildings of similar construction whenever possible, as relatively small modifications in detail — sizes of components, materials or wall profile — can dramatically affect the validity of the comparison. Nevertheless, this method provides the basis on which intelligent judgement can be made. Certainly the exposure grading set out here does bear an accurate relationship to the performance of existing buildings; and the driving-rain index is now being quoted in such documents as the British Standards Code of Practice CP 121: Part 1: Brick and block masonry, and in the Building Standards (Scotland) Regulations.

Two examples of observed correlation of the performance of building shells and exposure grading can be quoted. In areas classified as *sheltered* (up to 3 m²/s) a one-brick thick wall has been found unlikely to suffer from rain penetration, although it may well be unsatisfactory on other counts. Similarly a recent survey of dwellings in Scotland discovered that complaints of leaking windows were twice as frequent in areas of *severe* exposure (greater than 7 m²/s) as in areas of *moderate* exposure (3 to 7 m²/s).

It is important to remember that climate (particularly in the U.K.) can be very localised. Only 30 miles south of Glasgow and Lower Clydesdale (the only major urban area of the U.K. in the *severe* graded zone) palm trees grow at Culzean. It always pays to treat climatic problems with respect — and even with a certain amount of pessimism.

THE CONTROL OF WATER FLOW ON A BUILDING'S SURFACES

The way in which water flows over the surface of a building has not, until recently, been considered a subject worthy of study. In the past the traditional glossary of building details has saved the designer from having to consider very deeply what was really happening when rain deluged the surfaces of his buildings. He applied, more for aesthetic than practical reasons, the details his architectural training had taught him, although, in fact, most of the details had the very practical effect of breaking up concentrations of rainwater and spreading the washing effect of the rain more evenly over wall surfaces, thereby improving the weathering of the building.

It was only recently, after these details had been discarded in the 1930's search for a modern language of design, that weathering defects, which had not been noted before, became apparent; and the designer woke up to the fact that he had discarded more than traditional aesthetics. He began to appreciate that overhanging eaves, projecting copings, string courses and cills save buildings from the worst effects of the differential weathering associated with differing quantities of water flowing over the building surfaces. These differing flow quantities also create areas of potential leakage where water concentrations are high.

For the last forty years designers have been trying to come to terms with the conflicting requirements of producing 'modern' buildings which have clean, unfussy lines, and buildings which will not eventually become defaced by a totally arbitrary (from the design point of view) bas-relief of differential grime caused by the peculiarities of the water flow down the building's surfaces. Grime settlement is particularly noticeable in buildings of smooth, unfaced concrete. This material, when wet or dry, shows up the patterns of water flow more vividly than do traditional materials, whose texture, joint patterns and colours tend to disguise differential weathering. The secret of even weathering is an efficient *control* of the water flowing over a building's surfaces, the *dissipation* of water concentration and the *protection* of vulnerable parts of the building where water ingress is likely and would cause defacement. All three objectives are relevant to the problem of maintaining the weatherproof integrity of the building shell.

Roofs   The shapes of buildings, when allowed to develop unconfused by artistic cults, have always reflected the climate in which they were built. Vernacular building throughout the world has illustrated this perpetually. In wet parts of the world roofs were pitched, forming with their overhanging eaves a sound protection to the building below. This was an effective way of despatching rain quickly to a series of points outside the perimeter of the walls, from where it was disposed of by an external rainwater system. Such water as escaped this disposal system fell clear of the walls below and only reached the wall surface by being blown back in a diffuse shower of drops.

21

The pitched roof behind a parapet, however, was not an indigenous form in rainy areas. Its use was championed by the international Renaissance movement whose architects were trying to instill the spirit of Classical architecture, originally a Mediterranean form, into all new buildings whatever their location. It was an international cult, in much the same way as was the modern movement of the 'thirties', and aesthetic theory tended to over-rule local considerations. The pitched roof behind a parapet is not an efficient form in wet areas. Rainwater is collected inside the perimeter of the external walls, from where it is conveyed internally or externally to the drainage system. Any fault in the gutter results immediately in a leak which affects the building structure. What is more, the problem of creating a watertight gutter of this type is relatively complex. The form would never have developed as part of the vernacular architecture of wet countries; it was, in those areas, an imposed 'style' of building.

In the same way, the flat roof was an indigenous form of hot and arid areas of the world, where it was a part of their vernacular of building. It became generally adopted by modern movement architects because its use freed their plans from the strait-jacket of enclosing rectangles, which pitched roofs demanded. They strove for free-flowing plan forms, and the flat roof was the means of realising this ambition. They discarded the pitched roof, and by doing so gave rise to years of maintenance problems for their clients in high rainfall areas, because the technology of flat roof coverings was not at that time sufficiently advanced to be able to cope effectively with the problem. It is difficult to imagine how many of our complex and large-scale buildings today could be roofed in any other way than by a flat roof, and on major buildings the flat roof is certainly here to stay, but the back-up technology is now much further advanced. What should be understood is that this form is at variance with the vernacular tradition in high rainfall areas, and must be seen as a risk feature requiring particularly careful design.

In areas of heavy rainfall it must be accepted that to remove all water as quickly as possible from the plan area of the building is an ideal which should not be questioned. A rainwater disposal system which is situated outside the perimeter of the external walls will, obviously, create less risk than one that is predominantly internal. In the former, minor breakdown can be tolerated; in the latter, minor breakdown can cause major inconvenience to the occupants of the building. This, it could be argued, is an over-simplification, and in many ways it is; but it is a very real assessment of a practical risk. If the designer decides to take the risk, he must be sure his confidence — in the detailing of his building and the materials chosen for it — is not misplaced.

In precisely the same way, any roof which contains water rather than sheds it is a potential risk. Minor defects in the waterproof membrane, that would never be noticed if the water were not standing on the roof, become major disasters, often very difficult to trace. If the rainwater disposal system becomes blocked, the first hint that anything is wrong could be major leakage in many areas when the tray of the roof fills with water to a greater depth than the upstanding flashings.

The detailed discussion of such points as these is reserved for Chapter 4. Suffice it to emphasise here that design assessment needs to start with fundamental consideration of the way in which the shape of a building —

and particularly the roof – affects the likelihood of the ingress of water to the interior.

Walls

The modelling of the vertical surfaces of a building can affect the way in which water flows over its planes. As has already been mentioned, an eaves overhang protects the wall beneath. The head of a wall is a particularly vulnerable area, traditionally protected by an overhanging coping on top of a damp proof course. The coping throws the water clear of the wall; the damp proof course prevents damp penetration downwards through the coping (or the coping joints) and thence down the wall into the interior of the building. Today the dpc is there, but the projecting coping is often missing. Not only did the traditional coping give a strong emphasis to the head of the wall, particularly when viewed from below, but by the way it despatched water falling on its upper surface, concentrations of water were avoided which could otherwise have built up around irregularities on the top of the wall and spilt over in differential flow down the wall face. If the coping were correctly designed with sharp arrises and adequate throatings, the majority of the water would fall clear of the wall below, only a small amount blowing back as a diffuse shower of drops (Figure 1/6).

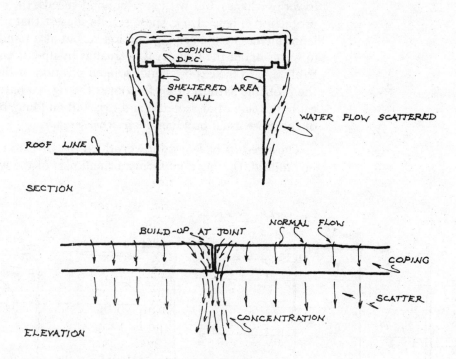

Figure 1/6 Water flow diagram – traditional coping.

It may be observed that this building up of rainwater at irregularities causes uneven flow on wall faces, and an irregularity can even be a joint in a coping. In other words, the point of risk can, itself, cause water build-up – hence the protective dpc under the coping. If the coping overhangs, such build-up from the joints is harmlessly dispersed; if the coping is flush (as is often the case today), whether of reconstructed stone, concrete or brick, festoon staining will be noted associated with the joint pattern. Whatever the cause, concentration of water on the face of a building is always undesirable. Even if there is no risk of leakage or decay, the differential weathering is unsightly.

23

Recent experiments carried out by the BRE have thrown an interesting new light on the way copings perform in conditions of driving rain. What has been noted above applies to water falling directly on top of the coping; but what is the effect of a coping on the disposition of driving rain on the surface below? In the natural test rig at Plymouth a series of readings was taken of rainwater catches below differently sized and placed overhangs on the rig wall. The lower overhangs acted completely as expected and provided considerable protection to the wall immediately below. In fact, where the projection was 200 mm or greater, protection was virtually complete, at wind speeds up to 20 m per second, for a horizontal joint positioned immediately below. The higher overhangs, however, produced different results. Here, catches were recorded often many times greater than catches recorded on the uninterrupted wall surface — catches generally increasing with windspeed and decreasing with increased depth of overhang. With a 50 mm higher overhang, the wall 50 mm to 175 mm below gave catches of driving rain many times greater than that on general wall surfaces. With 150 mm to 300 mm overhangs, this degree of increase was only recorded with wind speeds over 15 m per second. Up to 10 m per second the overhangs between 150 mm and 300 mm deep provided equivalent protection to the lower overhangs, but with greater wind speeds, the overhangs provided little protection (Figure 1/7). These results suggest that not only is local turbulence increasing the driving-rain index, but also raindrops are being driven upwards under the high level overhangs by up-currents of wind. This is probably due to the exposed and isolated position of the rig. Figure 1/8 shows the probable pattern of air flow over the rig — a pattern that could be typical in the case of an isolated and exposed building, but need not be typical of the more usual building in an urban area.

These results have not, however, led the BRE to recommend that copings be omitted. Driving rain is only a small part of the water reaching horizon-

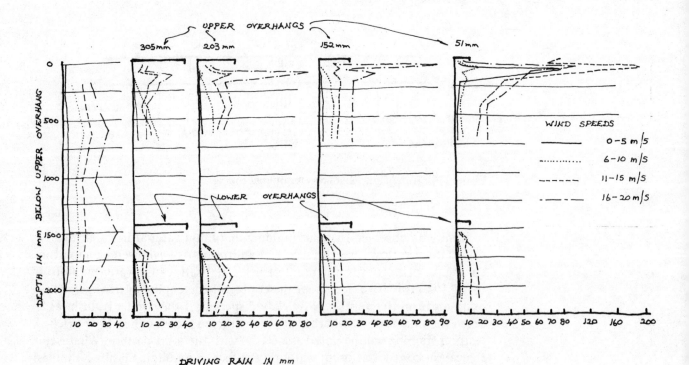

Figure 1/7 Graphs of protection from overhangs.

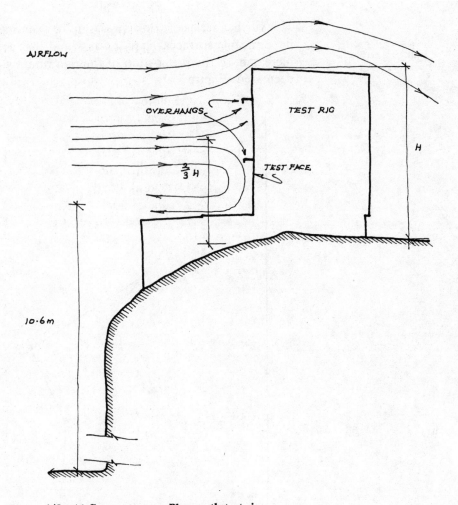

Figure 1/8   Airflow pattern – Plymouth test rig.

tal joints, the majority being run-off from walling above, or vertical rain. For these two, overhangs provide effective protection What the results do serve to emphasise is that parapet walls, or even the heads of walls in general, are high risk areas, warranting careful design assessment. It also emphasises that the traditional string course detailing in other positions on a wall can serve a very practical purpose by protecting horizontal cladding joints and similar high risk features.

Also associated with this test, readings were taken of rainwater catches some distance below the overhangs. These were found to be equivalent to those on normal unprotected walls, thus suggesting that water being thrown clear of the overhangs was not being blown back again.

BRE have also undertaken a study (as yet unpublished) of the run-off characteristics of rainwater on general wall surfaces. These have suggested that the high levels of water run-off previously predicted are not necessarily borne out by experimental results. A limited series of tests on four surfaces – concrete with exposed granite aggregate, concrete with a cement paint finish, rough board-marked concrete and London stock brickwork – has shown not only significant differences between materials, but also considerable variations in the ratio of theoretical to actual catch from the same material, due probably in part to different rates of absorption, wind directions and aerodynamic effects.

A further series of tests was set up to examine run-off on very smooth, impermeable surfaces. Here it was found that as the intensity of driving rain increased, so the proportion of the rain running down the wall actually decreased (Figure 1/9).

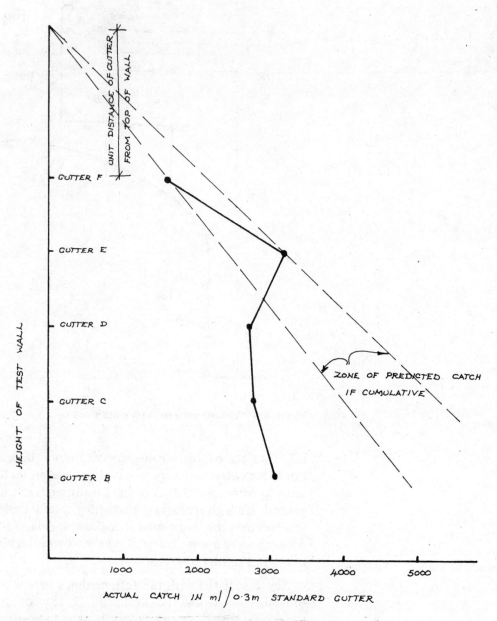

Figure 1/9   Run-off graph for smooth impermeable surface.

This phenomenon is not fully understood, but it is thought that some of the water running down the wall may tend to fall off, thus reducing the expected build-up quantity. The fact that as the intensity of rain increases, so the run-off becomes proportionately less suggests that the raindrop size has some effect on the results.

An experiment was set up to try to prove this fall-off theory. A series of horizontal collection trays was mounted normal to the test surface (Figure 1/10) and the catch in each 50 mm compartment was recorded. The resultant graph quite dramatically reveals a much higher collection of water just clear of the wall than on the wall itself. In fact, the catch tends to reach a

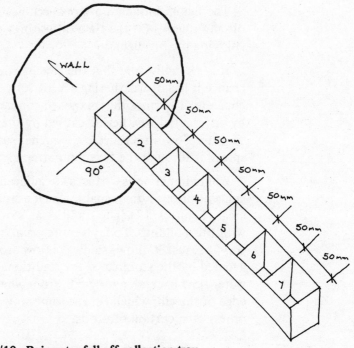

Figure 1/10 Rainwater fall-off collection tray.

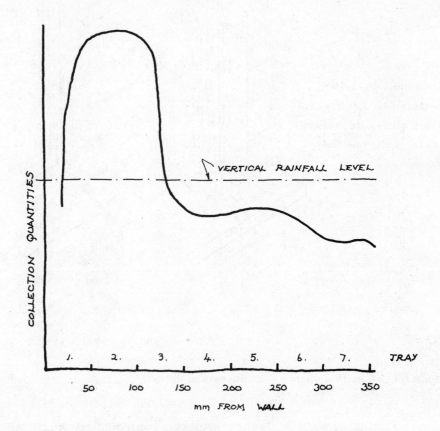

Figure 1/11 Graph of rainwater fall-off.

maximum at 100 mm from the test surface (Figure 1/11). It will be seen from the graph that collection at 100 mm from the wall is far in excess of the normal vertical rainfall level, while farther from the test surface the catch falls below the normal vertical rainfall level, indicating the sheltering effect of the wall.

There is still much more research necessary in the field of rainwater run-off and there is (at the time of writing) an international working party studying the problem.

It is generally true that the rougher the texture of a wall, the more chance it has of weathering successfully. This is particularly true of concrete. The smoother, exposed concrete finish quickly becomes streaked by differential weathering caused by the apparently arbitrary concentration of water flow on its surface. Rougher surfaces break up any water flow and spread it through the textural patterns.

Where impervious surfaces are adjacent to more absorbent ones, water concentration is unavoidable. Such a situation occurs at the base of glazed areas (Figure 1/12). The traditional, stooled window cill dealt effectively with this build-up. Today's more usual, non-stooled slip cill is less satisfactory, because it allows sideways flow around the edge of the cill, a defect avoided by the stooling of the traditional cill. The stooling turned the water flow back along the cill, from where it was despatched over the front edge of the cill, which (in the same way as the coping) spread it in a more or less even curtain of drops.

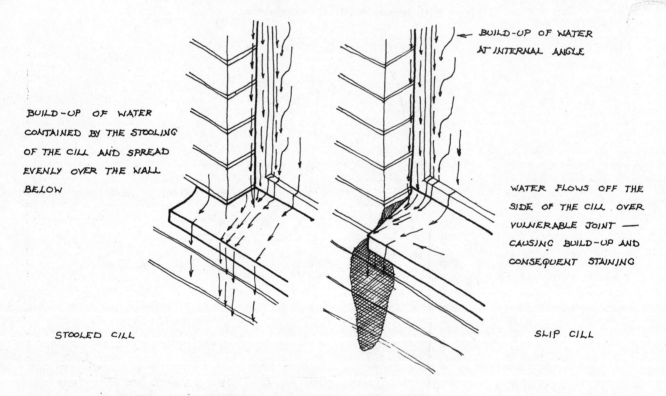

Figure 1/12 Waterflow diagram — traditional and slip cills.

In the pursuit of a contemporary vocabulary, the designer often makes his window an unmodelled hole punched in the wall. At the same time he shows a tendency to move the glass line forward towards the external surface of the wall. This in itself accentuates the risk of a leak developing, for deep reveals provide a surprising degree of shelter to the window itself and to the joint between the window and the wall. As water flow tends to concentrate at the edges of features, the jambs of glazed areas experience profuse water flow. If the reveal is shallow, there is a danger that this flow will be blown beyond the window area, with resultant staining of the outer face of the wall. The rainwater build-up at the window jambs must, therefore, be acknowledged and dealt with by careful weatherproofing of the joint between window and wall, by preventing moisture from by-passing the window through porous walling material at the jamb, and by dissipating the flow at the base of the glazing, clear of joints in the cladding or other points of risk. Where there are large areas of impervious materials (curtain walling, glazing, etc.) the water build-up creates major problems. Each side of every mullion becomes a race-way for water, which has to be directed safely away from vulnerable positions at the base. This problem, so often unresolved, is illustrated by tell-tale differential staining.

As explained in the last section, because of the local increases experienced in the driving-rain index at parapets or corners of buildings, due to local turbulence and consequently inflated wind speeds, these parts of a building become areas of risk. Joints in cladding should therefore be kept to a minimum, or eliminated entirely, at these positions. Corners of buildings also experience water concentrations in excess of those on the general wall surfaces. This is apparently due to the attraction of water to edges of planes, and its tendency to concentrate at any surface interruption. Tell-tale clean streaking illustrates this fact, particularly on buildings faced with exposed concrete. It is, therefore, recommended that vertical cladding joints should, wherever possible, be kept at least 200 mm from the corners of buildings.

The phenomenon of rainwater concentration at corners and surface interruptions has been studied by the BRE. Rainwater run-off has been measured and recorded on the surfaces of a buttress, and the data related to wind speed and direction. The water build-up at the corners was noted, to-

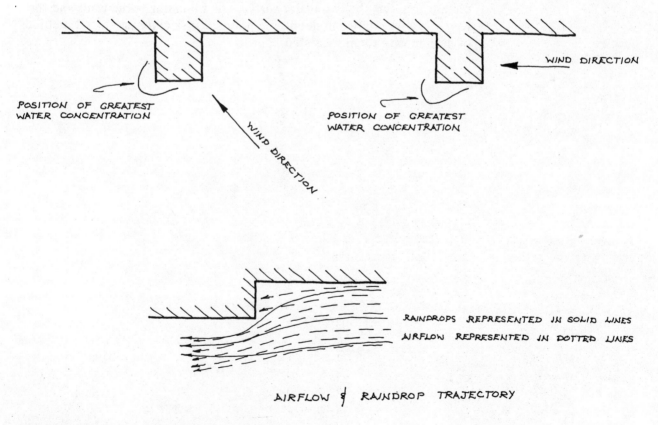

Figure 1/13 Rainwater concentration at corners.

29

gether with apparent relationships between degree of build-up on various corners and the wind direction. Often it was observed that the greatest concentration occurred not at the windward corner, but at the adjacent one. Similarly high concentration was often observed not on the windward surface of a corner, but on the adjoining surface (Figure 1/13).

This fact is related to the observed characteristics of water entry into vertical walling joints (see Chapter 3). Rain driven directly into a joint is rarely significant; it is rain being blown obliquely into the joint from the front face of the wall that causes the majority of rain penetration. It is for this reason that BRE recommend that a small shoulder or ridge should be provided at the vertical edges of wall panels to try to reduce this penetration (Figure 3/17). It has been claimed that side flow can be reduced if an exposed aggregate finish is used on concrete wall panels. BRE have checked this claim by carrying out tests in their Plymouth rig and in some cases have found it to be true, but results are not sufficiently consistent to be relied upon. The question of water entry into wall panel joints will be dealt with in detail in Chapter 3.

To summarise, it should be remembered that the subject of water flow over a building's surface is still not fully researched, and each designer must learn to appreciate which are the areas where water concentration is likely to occur on a building. This appreciation comes from making his own observations and applying current knowledge. He must then design building details which will dissipate the expected build-up of water either by casting it off the building, or by diffusing the flow as evenly as possible in places where it will not affect the weathertightness of the building. Often this is, of necessity, a question of logically analysing and thereby ultimately solving a problem, rather than of merely finding some ready-made solution. In succeeding chapters the two major surfaces of a building — the walls and the roof — will be studied in detail, the points of risk emphasised and methods of dealing with them suggested.

2 Standard Tests for Air and Rain Penetration

The penetration of walls by air and water can occur either through the joints between the elements making up the wall (between wall panel and wall panel, or between wall and door or window elements) or through the elements themselves (leakage through the walling or the windows).

BRITISH STANDARD TESTS

The British Standards Institution has laid down the basis for testing the degree of air and water penetration through walls and windows in BS 4315. Part 1:1968 of this standard deals with test procedures for windows and gasket glazing systems; Part 2:1970 with tests for permeable walling. These tests are fundamentally laboratory tests in which it is attempted to simulate actual site conditions of weathering and exposure. As a result, to some extent they fail in their intent. Simulation is never wholly satisfactory, but at least it forms a sound basis for comparative judgement between different systems, even if the results do not relate precisely to performance in use. On the other hand, natural weathering and exposure tests (as in the BRE rig at Staddon Height Fort, Plymouth, where the highest driving-rain index in mainland Britain has been recorded) have other limitations. Here the results are conditioned entirely by the exposure characteristics of the site of the rig. At Staddon Height Fort, meteorological data supplied by an adjacent meteorological station provides the basis on which the performance of walling elements on test in the rig is judged. For components tested in a laboratory, judgement is based merely on a comparison of one component with another, one result with another. Generally, however, it can be assumed that components producing better test results tend to perform better in practice. Experiments carried out by the Princes Risborough Laboratories to prove correlation between laboratory test results and performance in use will be discussed later.

It is now generally accepted that results given by the BS 4315 tests need careful interpretation. Experience in the use of the test apparatus helps in forming a balanced judgement of a specimen's likely performance in use. In some cases the test results are better than could be reproduced in practice; in some cases considerably worse. For instance, the effectiveness of the water penetration tests depends on the flow of water down the face of the walling specimen, and the severity of the conditions can be reduced, in the case of prefabricated panels, by the inclusion of an overhanging section at the head of the panel. Although in practice such an overhang would afford

31

substantial protection to the wall below, even from driving rain, in the test conditions the effect of such protection is grossly inflated. Conversely the dynamic conditions of the cyclic pressure tests for gasket glazing systems (Part 1, test C) are extremely arduous and the test results tend to be bettered in practice.

Apparatus

Both the window and gasket glazing tests (Part 1 tests) and the permeable walling tests (Part 2 tests) use basically the same type of test box. This is an airtight chamber with one face left open to receive the specimen to be tested. The structure of the chamber is such that it will withstand pressure in excess of the maximum test pressure and it is substantially the same as the chamber used by the working group on rain penetration of Conseil Internationale du Bâtiment (CIB). In addition to an access door, the test box is provided with one or more observation windows so that the internal face (weather-side) of the test specimen can be observed during the course of the tests.

Inside the box it is possible to produce an air pressure differential of at least 150 mm water gauge. The box is also equipped so that the difference between internal and external pressure can be measured to an accuracy of ± 0.5 mm water gauge, air entering the box can be measured to an accuracy of ± 2%, and it is possible to restore normal atmospheric pressure in one second and return to maximum pressure in three seconds.

Water is sprayed on the weather-side of the specimen in a horizontal band of approximately equal-sized droplets. In the case of Part 1 tests, the band must be 50 mm deep, having its centre line level with the centre of the highest horizontal bar of the specimen (Figure 2/1). In the Part 2 tests, the band is 250 mm deep and runs along the top of the test specimen. The rate

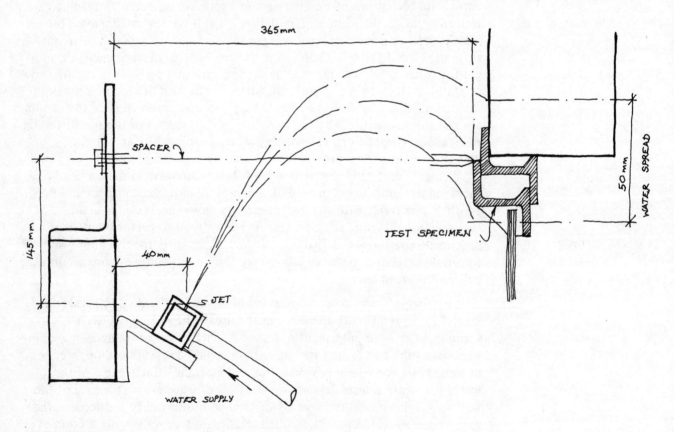

Figure 2/1 BS 4315 Water ejection pattern.

of flow for the Part 1 tests represents *"50 ml per minute for each 20 mm width of specimen"*; for the Part 2 tests *"25 ml per minute for every 10 mm width of test area"* – basically the same flow. Water is supplied to 20° C ± 1° C and, in the case of Part 1 tests, contains fluorescein sodium and a non-ionic, non-foaming wetting agent (the former, using a black light ultra-violet lamp, aids leakage detection).

The first test box of this type in Great Britain was developed by Crittall/ Hope in the 1960's; almost simultaneously similar test boxes appeared in other countries. The BS test box was largely based on the Crittall/Hope box and now there are approximately 40 test boxes in Great Britain, mostly owned by window manufacturers.

Specimens for testing in either Part 1 or Part 2 tests are to be as nearly as possible in the same condition as would be met in use.

Part 1 tests

Part 1 of the Standard deals with testing windows and gasket glazing systems. Three tests are described. Test A establishes air infiltration through windows; Test B the resistance of a window to water penetration under static pressure (applicable to putty and mastic glazing systems); and Test C the resistance of a gasket glazing system to water penetration under dynamic conditions.

Test A

The test specimen is placed in the open side of the box (the box being designed to contain a range of different sized specimens) and is sealed in position. All opening joints in the specimen are then sealed and the air pressure inside the box is raised by steps of 5 mm water gauge to a maximum of 100 mm water gauge. At each step the amount of air infiltration is measured. The pressure inside the box is then reduced in 5 mm water gauge steps and a similar set of readings taken. At each step the greater of the two readings is taken and all these readings form a set of 'blank' readings.

The test is then repeated with the sealing removed from the opening joints. When the 'blank' readings are subtracted from the final readings this establishes the degree of leakage at various differential pressures and is expressed in m³ per hour through each metre of opening joint and in m³ per hour through each m² of opening light.

This test, in effect, measures the amount of draught that can be expected through the opening parts of a window in various exposure conditions. It is assumed that major leakage will not occur from other parts of the window.

Test B

The test specimen is inserted in the test box as for Test A. Water is then sprayed on the inside (weather-side) face of the specimen, as previously described, continuously for 15 minutes and leaks are noted, using a black light ultra-violet lamp which aids detection due to the addition of fluorescein sodium in the water. The air supply is then switched on and the pressure in the chamber is raised in 5 mm water gauge steps (as in Test A), each step being held for 5 minutes, until *gross* leakage occurs, or a pressure differential of 150 mm is reached. Pressures at which *initial* leakage and *gross* leakage occur are noted. Initial leakage is defined as being the first sign of water penetration. Gross leakage is leakage of such a quantity that damage could be caused to the unit under test or the fabric of the building into which the unit might be installed, or inconvenience caused to the occupants of such a building.

Test C

This test is similar to Test B, but involves the cyclic imposition of pressure on the test specimen, rather than the steady pressure of the previous test. The purpose of the test being to assess gasket glazing systems, the opening joints of the window are sealed. The water spray is turned on and the air pressure in the box is increased to 15 mm water gauge and then further increased in 15 mm water gauge steps. At each step the pressure within the test box is returned to atmospheric pressure within 1 second, maintained at zero differential for 5 seconds, then built up again in 3 seconds and maintained at the differential pressure for a further 5 seconds. This cycle is repeated 20 times at each pressure step. Pressure is built up to a maximum of 150 mm water gauge. Initial and gross leakage pressures are recorded as before.

Part 2 tests

Part 2 of the Standard deals with testing the permeability of walling constructions. This is done in a similar test box to that used for the Part 1 tests and can be tackled in three ways. Method A records by time-lapse photographs the dampness on the rear (non-weather-side) of the specimen; Method B records the changed weight of the specimen after wetting during test; and Method C involves the collection and recording of the amount of leakage. In each case the test specimen is not less than 1 m X 1 m and to this is applied water, as specified previously, for periods of 1 minute at half-hourly intervals. The test continues for 48 hours with an air pressure in the box of 500 N/m² (50 mm water gauge) or the equivalent of a 29 m per second wind.

Method A

This method depends on the photographing of the white-painted external (in relation to the test box) surface of the specimen before the test commences and then again at half-hourly intervals — unless penetration is particularly rapid when the intervals can be shortened. As the dampness increases on this surface of the specimen, so its colour changes and is photographically recorded.

Method B

Method B determines the amount of water absorbed by the test wall by weighing it before the test commences and subsequently reweighing it at half-hourly (or longer) intervals. The increase in weight is expressed as a percentage of the dry weight. Clearly this test involves the easy detachment of the specimen from the front of the box for weighing and speedy replacement.

Method C

Method C records the quantity of water which leaks through the walling specimen and is collected on a dpc at its base over half-hourly (or hourly) periods until such time as the specimen is saturated. This is expressed in ml per m² per hour.

Clearly all the above tests are somewhat arbitrary. In spite of their being designed roughly to simulate exposure conditions encountered in practice, it is obvious that the test conditions are far removed from natural conditions. At best, as has been pointed out earlier, they provide a valid basis for comparative judgement of the performance of windows, or Type 1 walling, or individual panels of Type 2 walling. There is, however, no substitute for reliable in-use performance information, but this is invariably scarce.

Natural test rigs are slow in producing data because of the unpredictable nature of the British weather. Results derived from these sources, however, are likely to be more accurate and more directly related to the expected in-use performance of the test specimen than are results from laboratory tests. Having said this, it must be admitted that the laboratory tests provide indispensable and speedy information which could not be gathered in any other way.

An effort has been made by the Princes Risborough Laboratories to establish a correlation between laboratory test results and in-use performance. The Plymouth rig was used for this purpose, and into this were fixed 15 windows, covering 7 different types of construction, which had previously been subjected to laboratory tests. The Plymouth results tended to lack finesse, because it was impossible to keep a 24 hour watch on the rig; but the meteorological staff at the adjoining weather station took readings every day, which were related to their own data of rainfall and wind speed.

It was assumed that if the windows leaked they did so at the time of maximum pressure difference during the 24 hours period. The readings obtained were then compared with the laboratory test results and the graph in Figure 2/2 shows how highly significant were the results. The likelihood of a chance result of this nature is less than 1 in 1000. It seems, therefore, that the laboratory method, while imperfect, does provide a fairly good simulation of natural conditions.

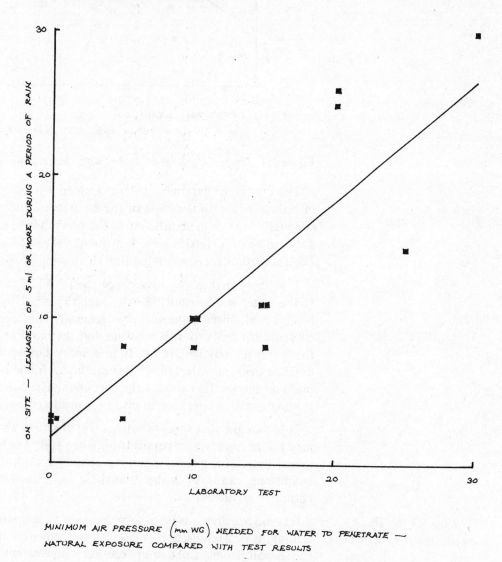

MINIMUM AIR PRESSURE (mm WG) NEEDED FOR WATER TO PENETRATE — NATURAL EXPOSURE COMPARED WITH TEST RESULTS

Figure 2/2 Water leakage — laboratory test and natural rig comparisons (PR Lab. Data).

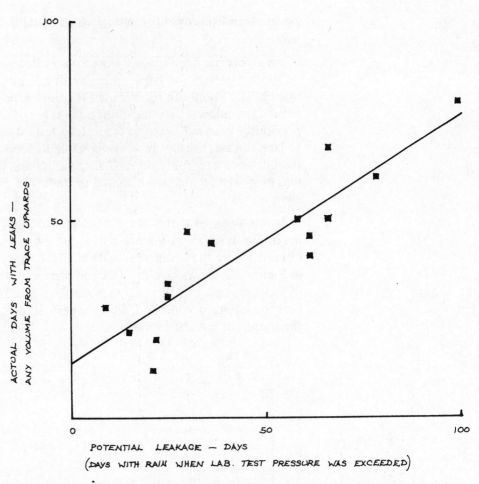

Figure 2/3 Predicted leakage compared with natural exposure leakage (PR Lab. Data).

The Plymouth data were then examined against the predicted frequency of leakage made on the basis of the laboratory findings, and these results (Figure 2/3) were as significant as the previous ones. Clearly more work needs to be done in this area; but the initial results appear to vindicate the BS test methods, at least regarding the testing of windows.

It is likely that in any revision of the BS 4315 the addition of fluorescein to the water will be omitted. Although this additive allows initial leakage to be detected, initial leakage is now generally considered to be without practical significance. Also, it is possible that the method of spraying water on to the specimen may be altered, an area spray similar to that used in German practice being substituted. In this method a frame of square patterned jets plays on the weather-side of the specimen. The Norwegian nozzle method (to be described later) might also be considered.

It is thought that some windows which satisfy the BS test requirements may fail to resist water penetration when tested at a lower pressure for a longer time. This phenomenon has already been noted in laboratory test conditions, and it is possible that these conditions more accurately simulate natural exposure.

The use of the BS apparatus for other tests

The BS apparatus is primarily designed to test windows and permeable walling. It is often used, however, to test other elements, such as joints between wall panels, and a study has been undertaken by the BRE to check the validity of such test results when compared with the results of natural exposure tests in their rig at Portsmouth (BRE Current Paper 81/74). The two-part drained joint recommended by the BRE for concrete panel joints, when tested in the BS pressure box, produced totally different results from those observed in conditions of natural exposure – for instance, if the air seal at the rear of the joint was effective, practically no water entered the joint at all. In the research reported in the Current Paper, water catches were recorded in plain-sided joints in the Portsmouth rig and the amount of water collected at different depths in the joint (measuring from front to back) were also noted. When the joints were tested in the BS pressure box the results were significantly different. It appeared that, if a water jet were aimed directly at a joint, there was a totally different result from that obtained when all the jets just missed the joint. Similarly arbitrary results have been claimed in the use of the apparatus when testing windows.

It would seem that the problem is associated with the method of delivering the water, since the present apparatus does not accurately simulate driving rain. Under natural conditions, most of the water entering a vertical joint is from side-flow from the adjacent panel face – a characteristic not reproduced in the BS apparatus.

The Norwegian test method (Norwegian Building Research Institute, Trondheim, Paper 0-2801) provides a closer simulation of natural conditions. Here the water is delivered by nozzles and is blown on to the test specimen by air jets mounted on a horizontal bar, which moves continuously up and down over the area under test. When the BRE applied this apparatus to the comparative joint test above, consistent and repeatable results were obtained, but less water was collected towards the front of the joint and more at the rear than in the natural exposure test. Although producing considerably better results than the BS equipment results, which showed no relationship to natural data, the Norwegian method is still not good enough.

BRE subsequently modified both test methods in an attempt to reproduce the natural test data. With the BS equipment more consistent results were obtained by inclining the test specimen at an angle of 1:4. The random pattern of the earlier results disappeared and the results more nearly matched those of natural exposure.

The nozzles of the Norwegian equipment were then angled at 30° to the face of the specimen – and the specimen was tilted at an angle of 1:4. Both modifications had the effect of producing drainage patterns very similar to those of natural exposure. It would seem, therefore, that the Norwegian apparatus would form a satisfactory basis for any future revision to the BS test box.

The important conclusion to be drawn here is that when any apparatus is being used to test features other than those for which it was designed, test results must be related to those of natural conditions before they may be considered satisfactory. Even when the designed test is being carried out it must be remembered that laboratory tests can be misleading if not interpreted with great care.

AGRÉMENT TESTS

One further set of tests used in the UK, which should be mentioned, are those included as part of the operations of the Union Européenne pour l'Agrément Technique dans la Construction, represented in this country by the Agrément Board. The Union Européenne consists of Belgium, France, Holland, Western Germany, Italy, Spain, Greece and Portugal, in addition to the UK, and it sets out its own methods of test for windows and doors in two documents, MOAT No 1 (Windows) and MOAT No 7 (Doors). These test methods are extended in exposure range for use in Great Britain, as explained in the Agrément Board Information Sheet No 1.

The Agrément tests, unlike the BS tests, are used to show the attainment of specific performance standards in the elements under test, in correlation with standards laid down by the Union. The BS tests, although they have been in existence for a number of years, have been backed merely by a performance document, Draft for Development DD4:1971 'Grading of Windows'. This will eventually be superseded by the appropriate Standard.

Basically the Agrément air and water penetration tests use a pressure box similar to the BS apparatus and they are in many respects similar to the BS Part 1 tests A and B.

Air penetration tests

A static pressure of 10 mm water gauge is produced in the pressure box and the volume of air passing the joints in the windows is measured. As with the BS test, only the opening sections of the element are considered as being tested. Fixed lights are assumed to be airtight. Therefore in calculating the surface area and length of joint only the opening parts are considered. The readings are expressed in m^3 of air flow per hour per m^2 of opening light. If the reading falls within the range $12 \, m^3$ to $60 \, m^3$, the test will be continued by measurements of the volume-flow at a pressure of 5 mm and 2 mm water gauge. If the reading is less than $12 \, m^3$, the test will be continued by measurements of the volume-flow at pressures of 25 mm and 50 mm water gauge. The Agrément performance standards will be discussed later in this chapter. Suffice it to say here that windows within the $12 \, m^3$ to $60 \, m^3$ per hour per m^2 range are considered as having 'normal' resistance to air penetration and those with less than $12 \, m^3$ per hour per m^2 as having 'improved' resistance to air penetration. Specific points of leakage are also tested by measuring each joint in turn.

Some members of the Union (particularly the Belgian STS) express maximum levels of air penetration in m^3 per hour per metre length of joint and not in overall area of opening light. Metal framed windows for instance under Belgian STS must achieve $6 \, m^3$ per hour per m without weatherstripping.

Watertightness test

Again, for water as for air, the same type of pressure box is used as in the BS tests. The Agrément Test is carried out in two phases. In phase one a water flow of 0.20 ± 0.05 litres per minute per square metre of test surface is introduced; in phase two the volume is increased to 0.75 ± 0.05 litres.

Air pressure rises in phase one are as follows:—

(a) 0 and 4 mm water gauge
(b) 0-4 mm and 16 mm
(c) 0-4-16-30 mm and 50 mm.

In phase two:—

(a) 0 and 4 mm water gauge
(b) 0-4 mm and 16 mm
(c) 0-4-16 mm and 30 mm.

Each pressure is applied for five minutes, with the exception of the first, which is applied for 15 minutes.

Windows are expected to resist *all* water penetration in each performance grade, but the UK interpretation allows minor leakage at the upper end of each performance range. At 50 mm water gauge pressure minor leakage, calculated as being not likely to cause damage, is permitted in the European standard. Windows and doors satisfying test conditions (a) are said to have 'normal' watertightness, (b) 'improved' watertightness and (c) 'reinforced' watertightness. These grades are related to exposure conditions, as will be discussed later.

Wind resistance test

Associated with the air penetration test is a strength test. In this, the sample is subjected to a pressure (first one side, then the other) of 150 mm water gauge and its deflection measured. This should not be more than 1/300. The air penetration test is then repeated to ensure that the results are no more than 5% worse than those before the wind resistance test was carried out.

Resistance to gale force winds test

This test is also associated with the air penetration test. Here the specimen is subjected to three successive, abrupt pressure rises to 100 mm water gauge (approximately equivalent to a wind speed of 150 km/hr) each held for three seconds. This is applied to both surfaces of the specimen and then the air penetration test is repeated to ensure that the results are still within 5% of those of the original test.

This brief assessment of those methods of test most frequently referred to will serve to explain the principles which will be mentioned again later. Throughout Europe and North America similar tests are used to establish similar data. Generally, West German and Scandinavian tests are more stringent while those in France and America are more lenient. There is at present an international committee meeting periodically to try to establish a European standard for windows and test methods used in their grading.

TEST METHOD IN THE USA

Static pressure testing of windows and curtain walling for air and water penetration in the USA is similar to UK practice. There is, however, in the States a method of test for water penetration employing dynamic pressure, which introduces a new concept into the testing of glazed elements.

Testing on a routine basis started in the States in 1950 at the University of Miami where equipment was used that was, in effect, a prototype of later dynamic test apparatus. An aircraft engine directed a blast of air at the specimen under test, while into the air stream water was injected to simulate driving rain. The method lacked sophistication, but at the same time the products being tested were themselves unsophisticated, since the standard specification for domestic windows allowed considerable leakage.

Early static pressure test methods were devised, using a pressure box with water that was supplied, originally, by a series of jets, and later (around 1958) – influenced by Norwegian techniques – by a grid of spray nozzles. The American Society for Testing and Materials (ASTM) finally, in 1970, issued a standard for testing water penetration of windows, curtain walls and doors by uniform static air pressure differential (ASTM E331-70). This was followed by a standard concerning the rate of air leakage through similar components (ASTM E283-73). The pressure box used in these tests is similar to the BS test box, but the method of applying the water in the water penetration test is by means of a grid of sprays. The rate of water application is 5 US gallons per hour per square foot – a rate equivalent to a rainfall of 200 mm per hour. This is clearly an excessive amount of water, particularly when applied to components intended for use in low-rise structures. The duration of the test is 15 minutes and the minimum pressure difference is 2.86 psf (13.75 mm water gauge) or the equivalent of 34 mph wind speed – a pressure too low for most high-rise applications. Usually designers specify a higher test pressure, expressed as a percentage of the design wind load. The Architectural Aluminium Manufacturers Association (AAMA) has high performance requirements for windows and doors which specify water testing at 10% of design wind load; while the National Association of Architectural Metal Manufacturers' (NAAMM) specification for testing curtain walls requires 20% of the design wind load with a minimum of 4 psf (19.23 mm water gauge). Most designers follow the NAAMM recommendations.

There is no ASTM standard for dynamic pressure test methods. These conform with NAAMM standard TM–1–68T 'Methods of test for Metal Curtain Walls' and involve the generation of a wind by means of an aircraft engine, equivalent to a static pressure of 20% of the full design wind load, and the application of water at a rate of 5 US gallons per hour per square foot. It has been noted that the dynamic test usually produces leakage at a lower pressure level than the static test, due to the higher impact of the water on the test specimen. The dynamic method has the advantage of producing a high frequency flutter, or vibration, in the specimen under test, due to uneven spillage of air off the specimen – a characteristic noted in components in use. This flutter becomes significant in large, thin glass or metal panels and can cause breakdown of seals used in gasket glazing. This test method is probably more effective than the BS test for gasket glazing.

The limitation of the dynamic test is the lack of standardisation of the test equipment. The pressure distribution across the face of the test specimen and the pressure differential, front to back, depend on the power of the wind generator and the size of the test specimen, yet each set of apparatus is probably unique. Many laboratories do not undertake dynamic pressure testing because of the cost of building the apparatus. In the UK the Royal Aircraft Establishment at Farnborough has been used by some gasket manufacturers to test their products dynamically up to wind velocities of 183 mph, but there is as yet no apparatus generally available for testing building components in an equivalent fashion to the American dynamic method.

The American static method offers more accurate control, although it does not produce any significant water impact on the test specimen, it allows unrealistic sheltering of certain parts of the specimen and it cannot create the pulsations that seek out areas of likely failure in joints subjected to the buffetting of the wind. These remarks can be applied equally to the BS 4315 Part 1 methods, except that Test C, involving cyclic pressure imposition, does to some extent provide an adequate alternative to the American dynamic pressure test.

PERFORMANCE STANDARDS

The BS 4315 and the Agrément test methods (as far as the latter apply to air and water penetration) have already been described. It was pointed out that there was one fundamental difference between these two methods. The BS method established a test basis, but did not relate this to performance requirements for the elements tested; the Agrément test, on the other hand, while using the same equipment applied slightly different methods in order to establish a direct relationship between the actual performance of the element tested and the performance requirements for such an element. The BSI in 1971 published a Draft for Development DD4 which set out to establish standards using the BS 4315 methods, but so far it has not been developed into a full standard. This is largely because an international committee, CEN, of which the BSI is a member, is endeavouring to establish a European standard for window performance. The British Standard has therefore been delayed so that it can be drawn up to accord with the international standard. The members of the committee, who represent Norway, Sweden, West Germany, Denmark, Holland, Belgium, France, Ireland, Spain, Portugal, Switzerland, Italy and Austria, as well as the UK, appear to be substantially in agreement. While the test methods in the various countries may vary, the results of the tests and the standards are often comparable. Certain countries, notably West Germany, Norway and Sweden, are particularly demanding in their requirements; France has test methods which are considerably less rigorous, so their standards are very much lower.

It seems likely that the eventual European standard will demand levels of performance not substantially different from those contained in DD4.

One further body has set down performance standards for windows. In 1970 the Interdepartmental Construction Development Group of the DOE, DES, DHSS and SDD published their Technical Note No 1 on Performance Requirements for Windows.

The standards of all three bodies have similarities, but differ with regard to the basis on which they assess the exposure of a building or site. The ICD Group base their air and water leakage standards on mean hourly wind speeds (Figure 1/2), BSI on maximum 3 second gust data (Figure 1/1), and the Agrément Board on a zoning map (Figure 2/4) prepared by BRE from Meteorological Office data and based on a statistical analysis of maximum three second gust speeds and maximum hourly mean wind speeds.

As wind speed is important in relation to the strength characteristics of the windows dealt with in the assessments of all three authorities, it is logical to use wind speed data for these calculations. Similarly, it is logical to use wind speed as a method of assessing air penetration; but as a basis for assessing exposure for water penetration, it seems less sound. Use of the driving-rain index map (Figure 1/3) might have appeared more reasonable, though high wind and rain are not necessarily always associated. However, as the driving-rain index is used only to assess exposure for rain penetration through permeable walling, and there is a much closer relationship between air and water leakage in glazed elements, to use wind data may not be as unreasonable as it at first seemed. As mentioned at the beginning of this chapter, there is fairly substantial evidence that laboratory test results on this basis are upheld by observed results in actual site conditions.

BSI defines three exposure grades: sheltered (40 m/s max. 3 second gust), moderate (45 m/s max. 3 second gust) and severe (50 m/s max. 3 second gust and above). Maximum air leakage is restricted to 12 m³/h/m length of

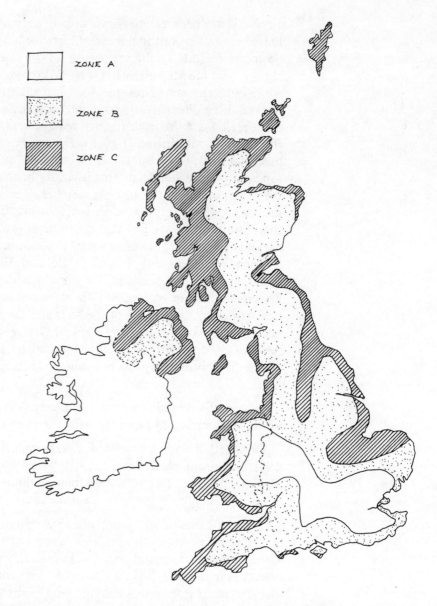

ZONE A

ZONE B

ZONE C

Figure 2/4   Agrément Board exposure zoning map (excluding Eire).

joint in opening lights for all grades, and this is verified by a 10 mm water gauge (sheltered grade), a 15 mm w.g. (moderate) or a 30 mm w.g. (severe) test. Gross water leakage (which could be defined as the amount of leakage that would be noticed and complained about) should not occur at pressures less than 5, 15 and 30 mm w.g. respectively at these exposures.

ICD Group sets out three exposure zones: 10.3 m/s, 12.7 m/s and 18.7 m/s mean hourly wind speeds. Again maximum air leakage in each zone is restricted to 12 m³/h/m length of joint in opening lights (or 60 m³/h/m² area of opening light) when the window is tested at 10, 15 and 30 mm w.g. for each exposure. No water leakage should occur at pressures of 5, 10 and 15 mm w.g. and no gross leakage at 10, 15 and 30 mm w.g. respectively in the three exposure grades.

Obviously there is a measure of compatibility between these two sets of requirements. ICD Group add a further requirement. The velocity of air leakage at any part of the window should not exceed 1.4 m/s. Both bodies refer to the necessity of judging local variations to the general exposure gradings, as do also the Agrément Board. All gradings assume no local shelter and are related to a height above ground level of 10 m in open countryside.

The Agrément Board exposure zones are designated A (normal), B (moderately severe) and C (severe). Air leakage for all zones should not exceed 60 $m^3/h/m^2$ of opening light when tested at 10 mm w.g. (equivalent of 11.2 m/s wind speed). Where air leakage is less than 12 $m^3/h/m^2$ of opening light, the window is designated as having 'improved' resistance to air penetration. With regard to water penetration, two pressures are designated within each exposure grade. At the lower figure there should be no leakage; at the upper figure there should be no excessive leakage.

Zone A – normal   4 – 16 mm w.g. ('normal' water resistance)

Zone B – moderately severe   16 – 30 mm w.g. ('improved' water resistance)

Zone C – severe   30 – 50 mm w.g. ('reinforced' water resistance)

Situations where various types of window may be used, according to height and degree of local shelter, can be stated as follows:–

Height of windows above ground

	Up to 10 m			*Up to 30 m*			*Up to 60 m*		
Shelter	*Nil*	*Low*	*Built-up*	*Nil*	*Low*	*Built-up*	*Nil*	*Low*	*Built-up*
Zone A	N	N	N	I	N	N	I	I	I
Zone B	I	N	N	I	I	N	R	R	I
Zone C	R	I	I	R*	R*	I*	S*	R*	R*

N = normal   S = special (outside 30 to 50 mm w.g. range)
I = improved   * = these exposure gradings may need special consi-
R = reinforced   deration

As previously noted, the Agrément Board lay down similar standards of air and water penetration for external door sets (MOAT No 7:1970). Doors tend to be overlooked with regard to weather exclusion, although this aspect of their design is often poor. The Agrément standards lay down precisely the same performance requirements regarding minimum air and water resistance for doors as for windows.

From the foregoing it will be seen that in the UK there are now two independent methods of assessing a window's performance, and window manufacturers can submit their products to either BSI or the Agrément Board to receive verification of their claimed performance. More and more manufacturers are taking advantage of these facilities, and designers would be well advised to make every effort to use windows with a test classification, particularly in the more exposed situations. This should remove one area at least of perpetual complaint about draughts and water ingress in exposed areas.

In the case of aluminium windows, a quality assurance scheme operated by the BSI has now been replaced by a kitemarking scheme based on BS 4873 which contains performance requirements. A number of members of the Aluminium Window Association already have windows which are kitemarked.

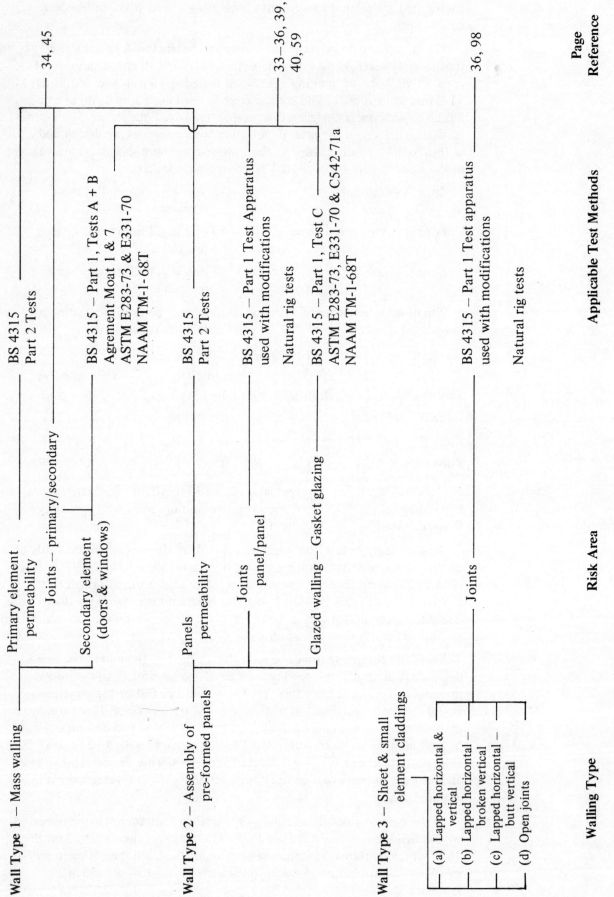

Table 3/1 Types of walling: risk areas and tests.

Walling Type	Risk Area	Applicable Test Methods	Page Reference
Wall Type 1 – Mass walling	Primary element permeability	BS 4315 Part 2 Tests	34, 45
	Joints – primary/secondary		
	Secondary element (doors & windows)	BS 4315 – Part 1, Tests A + B Agrément Moat 1 & 7 ASTM E283-73 & E331-70 NAAM TM-1-68T	
Wall Type 2 – Assembly of pre-formed panels	Panels permeability	BS 4315 Part 2 Tests	33–36, 39, 40, 59
	Joints panel/panel	BS 4315 – Part 1 Test Apparatus used with modifications Natural rig tests	
	Glazed walling – Gasket glazing	BS 4315 – Part 1, Test C ASTM E283-73, E331-70 & C542-71a NAAM TM-1-68T	
Wall Type 3 – Sheet & small element claddings	Joints (a) Lapped horizontal & vertical (b) Lapped horizontal – broken vertical (c) Lapped horizontal – butt vertical (d) Open joints	BS 4315 – Part 1 Test apparatus used with modifications Natural rig tests	36, 98

3 Walls and Secondary Elements

For the purposes of this book, walls have been classified in three types:—

Type 1 — monolithic walling such as in-situ concrete; also walling made up of an assembly of small blocks or units laid in and bonded together by jointing material (mortar) in such a way as to form one monolithic mass which is punctured by openings for doors and windows.

Type 2 — walling made up of an assembly of large, preformed elements or panels of like or unlike material, which are joined together to form a non-monolithic assembly containing glazed and/or solid elements.

Type 3 — walling made up of large sheet claddings or smaller lightweight claddings connected to a structural framework.

Type 1 walling includes brick, stone, concrete block and in-situ concrete walling; Type 2 precast concrete, timber or fibreglass-reinforced plastic (GRP) curtain walling and fully glazed walling; Type 3 corrugated asbestos or metal cladding, plastic cladding units and tile hanging.

In Type 1 walls it is the permeability of the walling materials themselves which is the most significant factor in the penetration of the structure by rain. Air and water leakage experienced where elements such as doors and windows occur are secondary failures and are dealt with in the Type 2 walling section where glazing systems are studied in detail. Walling of Types 2 and 3, being made up of less absorbent parts, has areas of risk sited almost wholly in the joints between elements, and additionally, in some examples of Type 3 walling, in the vicinity of through fixings. Table 3/1 highlights critical areas requiring special design consideration in each walling type. It also relates these areas, where possible, to BS 4315 Parts 1 and 2 (Methods of test for resistance to air and water penetration), Agrément Board and other standards.

MASS WALLING (TYPE 1 WALLING)
(Brick, stone, reconstructed stone, concrete block and in-situ concrete)

With the exception of in-situ concrete, Type 1 walling comprises small units laid to break joint and bound together by mortar. The impermeability of the wall is largely determined by the absorbency of the walling material, the character of the mortar and the skill employed in the laying of the walling units. Clearly, if the jointing material is porous, or hair-line cracks develop in the mortar, or between the mortar and the walling units, the wall will absorb some driving rain, even if the material itself is as impermeable as granite. Similarly, mortar joints which are not solid will assist the passage of water. While bedding joints are usually solid, due to the weight of the unit above, the perpends are often not thoroughly filled.

In addition to penetration of the main walling element, leakage can occur through the secondary elements (doors and windows), or at the junction between main and secondary elements. The secondary elements are discussed in a separate section, but those characteristics of the junction which are particular to Type 1 walling are dealt with in this section.

Main elements
All traditional walling materials are to some extent permeable. A material's absorbency very roughly correlates to the crushing strength of the material as is illustrated in the following table:—

Table 3/2   Properties of building materials

	Crushing strength (MN/m²)	Absorbency (% of dry weight)
Stone		
Granite	154	0.10
Limestone, Ancaster	59	2.5
Limestone, Bath, Hartham Park	13	11.6
Sandstone, Mitcheldean, Glos.	75	2.1
Sandstone, Robin Hood, Wakefield	30	10.0
Clay bricks (5 hour boil test as BS 3921)		
Staffordshire Blue (engineering)	(not available)	at least 4.5
Accrington Pressed	75.8	4.5
NCB Cannock wire cut sandfaced	51	6 to 7
Ibstock Aldridge Grey	65.5	8
Maltby Vandyke brown	65.9	12.1
NCB Desford wirecut rustic	31	23 to 24
Calcium Silicate bricks (sand-lime or flint-lime)		
Ibstock	20.6	16
Uxbridge flint facing	31	10
Uxbridge engineering	34 to 48	7 to 10
Reconstructed stone		
Aberdeen granite aggregate	50.2	4.6

It will be seen from the table that the harder stones demonstrate very little absorbency. These, however, are becoming increasingly rare in use, due to their high cost. Clay bricks vary substantially, from the hard engineering bricks which absorb so little water that they can be used, bedded in cement mortar, to form damp proof courses in walls of more absorbent materials, to the soft facing bricks which absorb water readily, but have a more pleasing appearance. Calcium silicate bricks have on average a much lower crushing strength, but relatively less absorbency. Reconstructed stone's characteristics vary largely according to the nature of the aggregate used in its manufacture.

In the past, sheer mass has been relied upon to prevent the ingress of driving rain through brickwork. This solution is no longer viable. Solid brick walls, untreated externally by waterproof rendering, have poor resistance to driving rain. A wall 327.5 mm thick is likely to perform reasonably well in sheltered or moderate exposures, but will leak in severe exposures. A 215 mm thick wall is only adequate in very sheltered positions. Generally, solid brick walls in severe exposures (and, if below 327.5 mm thick, in moderate exposures too) require an external waterproof rendering, or protection by tile hanging. Otherwise a cavity wall should be constructed. It is for this reason that almost all brick walls built today are of cavity construction. Exposure gradings in this context are derived from the driving-rain index referred to earlier.

The principle of cavity wall construction is the building of an air space within the wall. This air space prevents the passage of water from the wet outer leaf of the wall to the dry inner leaf. The amount of water penetrating the outer leaf will be directly related to the severity of the exposure, the absorbency of the facing brick and the quality of the jointing. Whenever the cavity is bridged, an impermeable layer or damp-proof course (usually of bituminous felt) is imposed between the wet and dry walling. In addition, horizontal bridging is provided with stepped flashings or cavity gutters which direct any water in the cavity away from the inner leaf and out through open perpends in the outer leaf (Figure 3/1). Wall ties of galvanized steel, stainless steel, plastic or copper are used to tie both leaves together and are spaced horizontally and vertically at intervals laid down in the Building Regulations. The ties are either of a flat strip or wire butterfly type to BS 1243 and are designed so as to discourage the passage of water along their upper surfaces to the inner leaf, a twist being formed in the middle of the tie for this purpose (Figure 3/2). The importance of keeping the cavity absolutely clear of mortar droppings and other debris can be readily appreciated. The build-up of mortar on a wall tie will provide a ready bridge for moisture transference across the cavity.

Argument has been raging for many years as to the advisability, or otherwise, of ventilating the cavity. If the cavity is ventilated, by placing air bricks at intervals along both the base and the head of the wall, the insula-

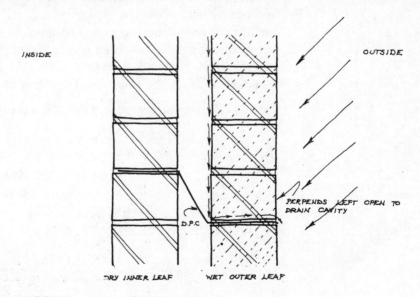

INSIDE

OUTSIDE

PERPENDS LEFT OPEN TO
DRAIN CAVITY

D.P.C

DRY INNER LEAF   WET OUTER LEAF

Figure 3/1 Principle of cavity closure.

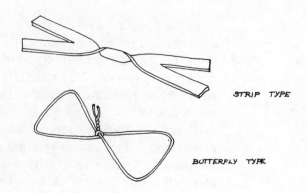

STRIP TYPE

BUTTERFLY TYPE

Figure 3/2 Wall ties.

ting effect of the air space will be reduced; on the other hand, the danger of excessive build-up of moisture, or the formation of condensation in the cavity will likewise be reduced.

On the question of insulation, the current tendency to fill cavities with foamed insulation (usually urea formaldehyde) can cause problems by reducing the efficiency of the cavity as a barrier to water penetration. In a free cavity the absorbed water flows down the inner surface of the outer leaf and drains away harmlessly below the external damp-proof course level. Cavity insulation obstructs this flow and increases the risk of rain penetration in some exposure conditions. In spite of the impermeable nature of the foam insulation, the fact that it obstructs the free flow of water makes it more likely that the water, following the line of least resistance, will reach any faulty cavity gutters and vertical dpc's and also cavity ties. In addition, if there are fissures in the foam — and these are very difficult to avoid, due to the foam's normal shrinkage — water may well pass through the fissure, using the foam as a bridge. Fissuring can be kept to a minimum by strict quality control of the raw materials.

The Agrément Board have carried out a survey of 11 093 installations of urea formaldehyde foam-filled cavities, during which it was discovered that rain penetration occurred at the rate of 1 in 38 cases in conditions of severe exposure, and 1 in 50 in conditions of moderate exposure, whereas no cases occurred in sheltered conditions. Of the 1 508 installation carried out in accordance with Agrément Board recommendations (that is, restricting the use of cavity insulation to sheltered areas, or buildings up to 2 storeys in height on moderately exposed sites with some local shelter) only one failure was recorded. It would, therefore, seem that the Agrément Board recommendations should be followed. These can be tabulated as follows:—

Table 3/3 Recommended usage of foam-filled cavity wall construction

Exposure (driving-rain index)	Recommendation
Sheltered	Risk of penetration insignificant
Moderate (with some local shelter from surrounding structures)	Safe up to 2 storeys
Moderate (no local shelter)	Cavity insulation not recommended except with addition of protection to outer surface
Severe	of the wall.

Recently the NFBTE, BRE, Agrément Board and the National House-Building Council (England and Wales) have issued a Guide to the Use of Urea Formaldehyde Foam for Cavity Insulation in New Construction which produces admittedly conservative recommendations, but ones which should be observed pending more detailed driving-rain data. This guide relates the materials comprising the outer leaf of the cavity wall to exposure zones. Materials are divided into three classes:—

Class A Brickwork or blockwork with reasonably crack-free rendering, or walling with weatherproof cladding.

Class B Average quality clay brickwork with reasonably filled joints.

Class C Non-absorbent materials (e.g. reconstructed stone, dense brick or dense concrete blocks).

In addition, the guide subdivides the geographical exposure zones according to local conditions, each zone being divided as follows:—

Protected — surrounded by many buildings or protected by heavy trees or buildings within 10 metres

Medium — in the middle of generally built-up or wooded area with open spaces extending more than 10 m and up to 100 m from the building in question.

Exposed — surrounded by open ground for a distance of 100 m to 1 km.

Very exposed — surrounded by open ground for more than 1 km; or locally high situation with extensive views.

The resulting recommendations are represented in Table 3/4.

If the wall to be insulated faces well away from the prevailing driving rain direction (usually between south and west, but not invariably) the local exposure grade can be relaxed by one grade. Conversely, it should be increased by one grade if the building is within 8 km of the south coast.

Table 3/4 Guide to the outer-leaf walling materials required in urea formaldehyde foam-filled cavity wall construction

Geographical exposure	Local exposure			
	Protected	Medium	Exposed	Very exposed
Sheltered	ABC	AB	AB	A
Moderate	AB	AB	A	A
Severe	AB	A	A	A

The guide recommends that urea formaldehyde foam insulation should not be used in any exposure conditions when the cavity wall is constructed of dense, perforated bricks, or blocks with raked joints, unless such walls are rendered, or protected by other waterproof cladding. In addition, guidance is given on standards of constructional workmanship and detailing, particularly relating to cleanliness of the cavity and damp proof courses and cavity gutters.

It is inferred that cavity insulation making use of other materials such as Rockwool or Rocksil slabs and Expanded Polystyrene would require less onerous restrictions, but no recommendations are given. To ascertain the conditions under which these materials could be safely used the appropriate Agrément Certificate should be consulted.

It must be emphasised that cavity insulation does make a significant reduction in heating costs (up to 30% in a typical dwelling), but the dangers of rain penetration should not be ignored. In addition, the filling of cavities appears markedly to reduce the sound insulation characteristics of the wall, due to increased flanking transmission. This can have unfortunate effects adjacent to party walls – or in the party walls themselves, where insulation would appear to be positively undesirable.

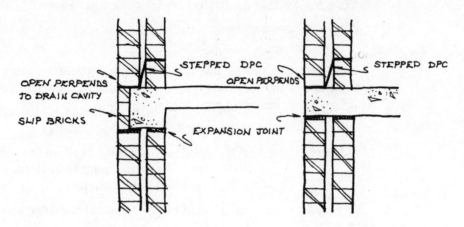

Figure 3/3   Brick cladding to framed structure.

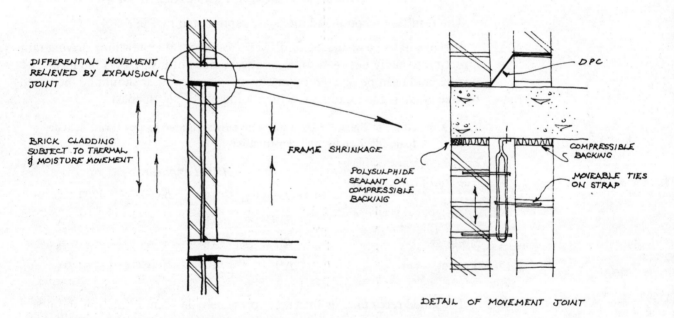

Figure 3/4   Movement joint in brick cladding.

Cavity construction is not restricted to loadbearing walls, it is also commonly used for the brick cladding of framed structures. Again, the same principles apply (Figure 3/3). To avoid failure or cracking of the brickwork, the possibility of differential movement between the cladding and the structure should be appreciated. This differential movement could be caused by thermal expansion or by changes in moisture content. Movement joints should, therefore, be incorporated in the design. Such joints are usually placed at the head of each storey-height lift of brickwork (Figure 3/4). They are formed of a material such as a polysulphide sealant, which will remain flexible to accommodate future movement without loss of adhesion to the adjoining materials. This subject is dealt with in more detail later (see *Choice of jointing material or seal,* pages 76–78).

Concrete blockwork

Cavity walls need not be constructed wholly or even partly of brickwork. For a considerable time it has been the practice to use blockwork for the inner leaf, and now it is becoming increasingly common to use blockwork for both leaves.

Single leaf block walls, as with solid brick walls, are difficult to make watertight without external protective treatment. Even if the blocks and the mortar are impermeable, slight movement can cause fine cracks or capillary channels through which moisture travels. We shall see in Type 2 walling joints that it is unwise to rely on a one-part joint. A single leaf block wall places the same reliance on perfect workmanship and materials.

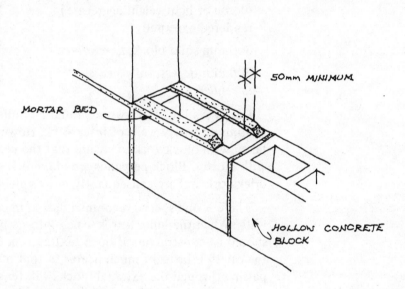

Figure 3/5 Shell bedding.

Single leaf walls at least 200 mm thick, if treated externally with a waterproof rendering, will successfully resist the ingress of water. Their performance can be improved if a hollow block is used and the horizontal bed joints are not filled continuously across the width, but consist of two separate 50 mm wide strips, one at each face (Figure 3/5). This technique is known as shell bedding and makes the joint less vulnerable to the passage of water, but reduces the loadbearing capacity of the wall by three quarters. A 200 mm thick wall of hollow blocks so treated and without external rendering could be expected to remain watertight up to and including moderate exposures.

The resistance of single leaf concrete walls to rain penetration can be tabulated as shown overleaf.

From Table 3/5 it is obvious that in many cases cavity construction is the only safe form, unless some type of external protection, such as rendering, tile hanging, etc., is to be applied.

Table 3/5 Guide to the use of single-leaf concrete walls

Type of wall	Recommended usage in differing exposure grades		
	Sheltered	Moderate	Severe
Min. 250 mm solid aerated blocks with external rendering	Yes	Yes	Yes
Min. 200 mm hollow blocks (dense or lightweight aggregate) shell bedded + rendered externally	Yes	Yes	Yes
Min. 200 mm solid aerated blocks rendered externally	Yes	Yes	No
Min. 200 mm hollow blocks (dense or lightweight aggregate) shell bedded, *unrendered*	Yes	Yes	No
Min. 100 mm solid blocks (dense or lightweight aggregate) rendered externally	Yes	Yes	No
300 mm solid block, *unrendered*	Yes	No	No
200 mm or less, fully bedded, *unrendered*	No	No	No

Cavity walls of blockwork should be built following the same principles as apply to cavity walls of brickwork. However, even greater care must be taken with blockwork to ensure that the perpends are thoroughly filled with mortar. Block perpends are individually much longer than those in brickwork and are consequently more vulnerable.

There is one special recommendation in connection with block cavity walls. When the inner leaf is sealed internally with plaster, the outer leaf should be constructed of open textured blocks. In this way air pressure in the cavity is brought much nearer to that of the outside air, and any air passing through the external blocks will tend to deposit whatever water it is carrying on the irregular surface of the blocks. If the external leaf is of denser, less permeable blocks, the rain could be forced through hair cracks between the blocks and the mortar aided not only by the wind but also by the air pressure differential between the windward face of the wall and that of the cavity.

Mortar

Mortar used in conjunction with bricks or blocks should be chosen not only from the point of view of its strength, but also bearing in mind the exposure conditions which the mortar, no less than the walling material, has to withstand. A correct choice of mortar will have a significant effect on the resistance of the wall as a whole to rain penetration.

It has been established from work by the BRE and the National Research Council of Canada that the initial rate of absorption of the brick and the water-retaining capacity of the mortar combine to affect the permeability of the wall. The greater the initial absorption of the brick, the higher the wall's permeability; but the use of a mortar of greater water retentivity can markedly decrease this permeability. Water retentivity of the mortar can be increased by the addition of lime or a plasticiser, such as cellulose ether.

Table 3/6   Recommended mortar mixes

Normal construction above dpc, not to withstand heavy loads	*Sheltered or moderate exposure*	*Severe exposure (or autumn and winter conditions)*
Clay bricks	1:2:8 or 9, cement:lime:sand 1:8, cement:sand + plasticiser 1:3, hydraulic lime:sand	1:1:5 or 6, cement:lime:sand 1:6, cement:sand + plasticiser 1:2, hydraulic lime:sand
Concrete blocks	1:2:9, cement:lime:sand 1:8, cement:sand + plasticiser	1:1:6, cement:lime:sand 1:6, cement:sand + plasticiser

Normal construction but in parapet walls, below dpc, or in free-standing walls	
	Mixes as for severe exposure above
Clay bricks over 34.5 MN/m² crushing strength	1:3, cement:sand

Also, resistance to water penetration can be improved in walls constructed of absorbent bricks if their initial high suction can be reduced by thorough wetting before laying.

In-situ concrete

In-situ concrete represents a completely different problem. This is the only walling in this category that is truly monolithic. If the structure is correctly designed, and care is taken to divide the wall into sections by construction and expansion joints, the wall should present a perfect and jointless face. Concrete is a relatively impervious material. The more impervious it is, the better it weathers. It can never, however, be totally impervious, because of the inescapable presence of voids, but these can be minimised by avoidance of:–

(a)   excessively wet concrete mixes

(b)   incomplete curing, or allowing to dry out during hydration

(c)   trapping air in the concrete during mixing or placing.

Paradoxically, the use of an air entraining agent can decrease the porosity of concrete. It is the character of the voids, rather than the mere presence of voids, which affects the permeability of concrete. The *controlled* introduction of air bubbles into concrete dramatically increases its resistance to water penetration. For this reason, concrete exposed to alternate cycles of wetting and drying should always be air-entrained.

Methods of testing the absorbency of concrete are laid down in BS 1881: Part 5:1970. *Initial surface absorption* is measured by determining the rate of flow into concrete per unit area after a stated interval from the start of the test and at constant temperature and applied head. *Water absorption* is measured by completely immersing a dried concrete specimen in water for a specified time and expressing the resulting increase in weight as a percentage of the dry weight of the specimen. The type of aggregate markedly affects the result of such tests. Here are a few typical results:–

Table 3/7   Absorbency of concrete

Type of aggregate	Initial surface absorption $10^{-2}ml/m^2s$				Water absorption % of dry weight		
	10 min.	*30 min.*	*1 hr.*	*2 hr.*	*30 min.*	*24 hr.*	*48 hr.*
Gravel	6.6	5.0	2.8	1.1	2.4	6.1	6.7
Limestone	6.5	4.5	2.5	1.0	2.8	6.2	6.4
Sintered PFA	12.5	10.0	5.8	4.2	8.4	14.5	15.0

53

Secondary elements: junctions

Secondary elements (doors and windows) in Type 1 walling cause two regions of risk with regard to air and rain penetration. The secondary elements themselves may leak (and because these elements may be equated with the glazed elements in Type 2 and 3 walling, consideration of their performance is postponed to the section on Type 2 walling), and the joint between the walling and the secondary element may allow air and rain penetration.

The junction problem is associated both with the position of the door or window frame within the reveal and with the sealing of the joint between dissimilar materials. The position of the frame in the depth of the reveal in solid construction is vital if damp patches are to be avoided adjacent to the back of the frame. Not only does a deep reveal shelter the secondary element, but as the impermeability of the walling material is being relied upon to maintain a dry interior, the frame should be placed deep enough in the reveal to be backed by dry walling (particularly if the element is of timber).

There remains the danger of dampness bridging behind the frame from the wet material of the outer reveal (Figure 3/6). In the case of cavity construction the vertical dpc should form a complete and effective division between the wet and dry walling material, and the position of the frame of the secondary element should be associated with this dpc in such a way as to avoid moisture bridging the membrane.

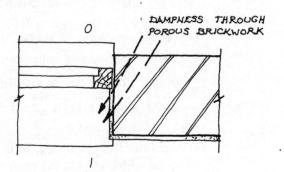

Figure 3/6 Window jamb in solid wall – bridging by rainwater.

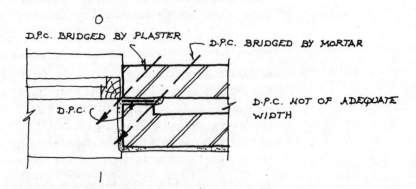

Figure 3/7 Window jamb in cavity wall – bridging by rainwater.

There are two major causes of dampness at the jambs of secondary elements in cavity wall construction:–

(a) bridging of the dpc by moisture from the outer leaf can occur either within the cavity via mortar droppings, or at the reveal via the plaster (Figure 3/7).

(b) shrinkage of the frame away from the walling (Figure 3/8).

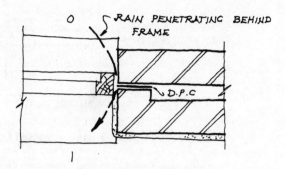

Figure 3/8   Window jamb – shrinkage gaps.

Ideally the dpc should be wide enough to avoid bridging in the cavity and to lap with the frame. In other words it should not be the exact width of the cavity closer, as is so often the case. The lap with the frame, if it can be achieved, will also help to eliminate problems of penetration due to shrinkage. The elasticity of the sealing compound at the front of the joint should be sufficient to accommodate any shrinkage likely to occur.

The position of a window frame in relation to the dpc is a controversial matter. The standard timber window frame, when used without a subcill, must be positioned with its inside face in line with the back face of the outer skin of the cavity wall, if its cill is to be effective. This is not an ideal position. Bridging of the dpc can occur, unless the dpc is able to be held firmly in contact with the back of the frame. Also the whole of the timber frame backs on to potentially wet brickwork of the outer leaf, which could, in exposed areas, lead to rot.

A better detail is achieved by moving the frame further towards the inside of the building, so that it straddles the dpc. The back of the frame is

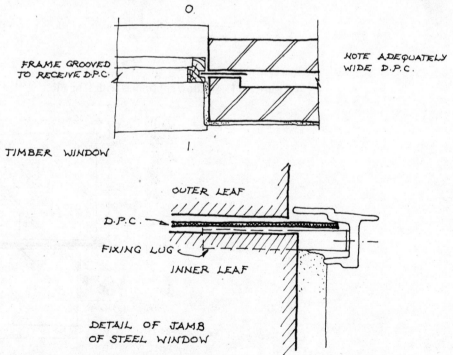

Figure 3/9   Window jambs straddling dpc's.

55

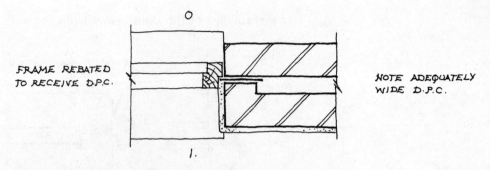

Figure 3/10 Window jamb — rebated frame.

then grooved to receive the dpc (Figure 3/9). Provided that the dpc is truly located in the groove (and this depends on good site supervision), the detail works well. Some form of subcill will, however, have to be used. The same effect can be achieved by rebating the jamb (Figure 3/10).

Some British steel sub frames are provided with a long nib which can be used in place of, or in conjunction with, a dpc (Figure 3/11). Some American metal frames follow the same principle.

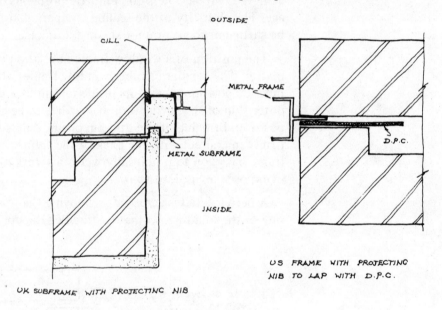

Figure 3/11 Window subframes with long nib.

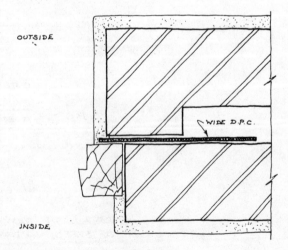

Figure 3/12 Window jamb — Scottish variety.

Scottish practice is to set the inner leaf back to receive the frame with the dpc overlapping the front face of the frame (Figure 3/12). This has the advantage of the frame being backed by dry walling and the window being sheltered by deep reveals — a significant advantage in areas of high exposure. However, closing the cavity to the back, rather than the front, demands the use of an extra wide dpc to avoid rear bridging. Also the detail can be rendered unworkable by today's narrow, standard window sections.

Figure 3/13 shows some recommended methods of handling the dpc at window heads and cills.

The external joint between walling and a secondary element has been traditionally undertaken in mortar. Because of the differential movement of dissimilar materials and the non-elastic nature of mortar this seal eventually tends to crack. Today this joint is undertaken by a sealing compound

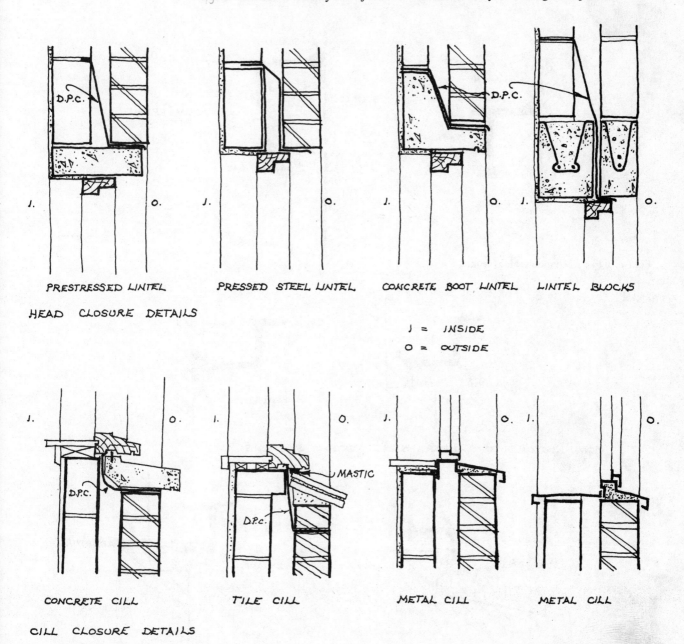

PRESTRESSED LINTEL   PRESSED STEEL LINTEL   CONCRETE BOOT LINTEL   LINTEL BLOCKS

HEAD CLOSURE DETAILS

J = INSIDE
O = OUTSIDE

CONCRETE CILL   TILE CILL   METAL CILL   METAL CILL

CILL CLOSURE DETAILS

Figure 3/13 Head and cill details.

(referred to generally as a mastic joint) whose ability to remain elastic within certain limits qualifies it to provide a long-lasting seal between walling and secondary element. The ease of gunning a satisfactory seal into place must be considered in the design.

It must be possible to use the gun even behind easy-clean hinges. The seal should be gunned into a well defined space with definite edges and firm backing so that a seal consistent in both width and depth is achieved. Typical details often do not satisfy these conditions and the mastic seal is an ill-defined daub between two right angled surfaces (Figure 3/14). The BRE has recommended, in CP 86/74 (Figure 3/15), modifications and adaptations to standard frames to provide better profiles for a sealant joint. The increased cost of such joints due to the greater quantities of sealant used would be counteracted by the improved efficiency and life of the joint.

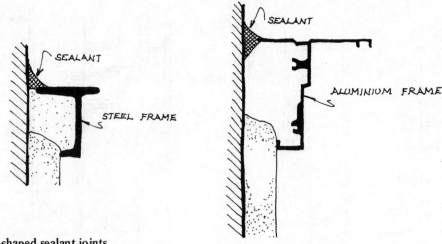

Figure 3/14   Ill-shaped sealant joints.

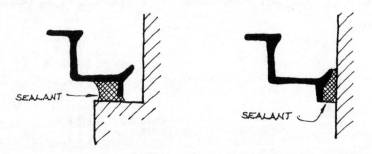

MODIFICATIONS TO STANDARD STEEL WINDOW SECTIONS

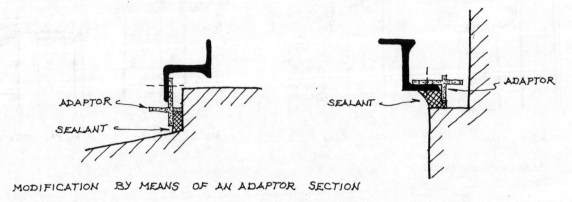

MODIFICATION BY MEANS OF AN ADAPTOR SECTION

Figure 3/15   BRE recommended adaptations of frames for sealant joints (CP 86/74).

58

A sealant is not likely to have a life expectancy as great as that of the building on which it is used. Joints should, therefore, be capable of inspection and replacement at the expiration of the sealant's life. In the section on Type 2 walling, later in this chapter, there is a comprehensive list of sealant types from which a choice of the correct sealant can be made.

Secondary elements: design defects

Finally, defects other than faulty joints between the walling material and the secondary element can lead to dampness in a window or door reveal. In determining the cause of dampness in any situation it is best not to jump to the most obvious conclusion. The real cause is often far from obvious.

Condensation on the glass or the metal frame can be misinterpreted as leakage. Drainage channels should be provided in the window design to remove this condensation. Within hollow metal frames a sufficient quantity can be formed to saturate sizeable areas of wall. This quantity will be substantially reduced if the frame is filled with a vapour-impermeable material, but in certain circumstances this can prove difficult to achieve. Where hollow frame members are used without filling, the detail should be such that any condensation that occurs will be led outside the building.

Defects may be present in the frames themselves, as described in the following three examples relating to timber, steel and aluminium windows respectively.

There is a practice of allowing the water check grooves in timber jambs and mullions to pass through the cill on the sides of tenons or comb fingers. This is to be deplored. It clearly results from a desire to simplify the timber machining, but nevertheless it provides a ready path for water to penetrate to the walling below.

The manufacturers of some standard steel windows, in an effort to make their products universally applicable, produce sash rebates punched for a variety of fixings and fittings. Some of these punchings will not be used in practice, and if the unused holes are not filled in the made-up window they can provide entry points for water.

Corner joints of aluminium windows are a potential point of leakage. Flash butt welded corners are rigid and waterproof, but require cleaning and polishing — an expensive additional operation — and will show through anodising. As a result, other methods of connection are sometimes used which are not as satisfactory and can be disrupted in handling or fixing. If this is likely to occur the section should be detailed to lead out of the building, by extending and stooling the cill, any water penetrating the corners.

Each of these frame failures could show up as rain penetration through the wall-to-window joint, examples emphasising that it is often difficult to find where the fault lies. The supposedly obvious answer is not always the right one.

WALLING ASSEMBLIES OF PRE-FORMED PANELS (TYPE 2 WALLING) (Precast concrete, timber, or GRP wall panels etc., curtain walling and fully glazed walling)

This walling type is a non-monolithic assembly of large pre-formed parts, all of which demonstrate a high degree of impermeability. Even the precast concrete panels are usually designed so that backing is not necessary to produce a watertight wall. Thermal insulation is usually provided as an integral part of the wall panel or (in the case of curtain walling) infill panel. Although backing walls may be required, particularly behind curtain walls, for Building Regulation requirements this demand is not connected with the weatherproof characteristics of the walling system. Many examples of this form of walling are typified by their ability to provide a fully finished external face, thermal insulation, and a smooth internal face suitable for direct decoration.

Because the walling elements are basically impermeable, the risk area in Type 2 walling is centred entirely on the joints between the elements, whether they are joining like materials or dissimilar materials. In the case of fully glazed walls, the problem is also associated with the overall window design and the prevention of draughts and water leakage through glazed walling elements. Consequently, we will first deal with the design of joints between major walling components, and then with glazed elements.

Joint design principles

The primary objective of a joint between walling components is to exclude water as effectively as do the components themselves. Today, walling components are relatively impermeable, thereby expeditiously discharging rainwater down their surfaces and placing more risk on the joints between the walling components. Because of a lack of precise information on the effectiveness of previous joint designs, there is a tendency to base new designs on test data, which may or may not accurately reflect conditions which will be met with in use.

Traditionally, the detailing of joints was not considered worthy of special attention. The wall was made up of a series of small components of fairly absorbent material and both the joint and the walling components relied on their thickness, or an in-built cavity in the wall construction, to prevent the moisture on the outer surface from penetrating to the building interior.

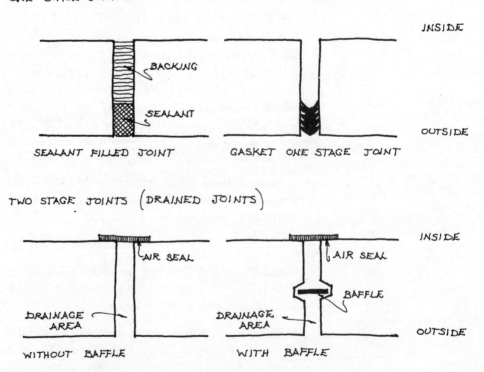

Figure 3/16 Sealant filled joint, one stage gasket joint and drained joints.

Until recently joints were treated as one-stage devices. The components to be joined were sealed together by a sealant medium at, or near, the front face of the components. If the sealant cracked, or separated from either component, failure occurred. There was no secondary line of defence.

Today, where the depth of the components to be joined is great enough, the two-stage approach is often employed. In this, an effort is made to prevent the weather from making direct contact with the sealant by designing the shape of the joint to give protection. By placing the sealant deep within the wall thickness, with a drainage area in front of it, most of the water entering the joint drains away without touching the sealant. Figure 3/16 illustrates the two techniques.

The weathertightness of a joint is directly associated with the leakage of air through the joint. If air leakage occurs, water is liable to be carried through the joint, unless its passage is baffled effectively within the depth of the joint and it is allowed to drain away towards the outer face of the building. Clearly the air leakage rate is a function of the difference between the air pressure at the front of the joint and that at the back of the joint. This pressure difference is brought about by the local wind speed. The success or failure of a joint, therefore, depends to a great extent on the air-tightness of its sealing, the force with which the air pressure drives the water inwards and the effectiveness of gravity in inducing that water to drain downwards through the open drained joint.

It should be remembered that the number of *raindrops* which are driven directly into a joint is relatively small. The greatest potential danger arises from the water which flows down the surface of the wall and from there is driven into the joints. This is known as side flow, and it can be reduced by designing the panels with shoulders or projecting ridges along their edges (Figure 3/17). The importance of considering how water may be expected

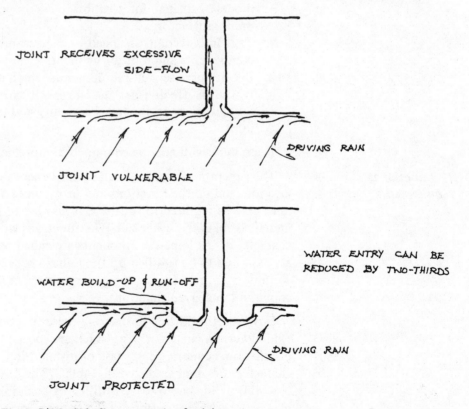

Figure 3/17 Side-flow protection for joint.

61

to flow over a building's surface and how it may be dispersed and thrown off have already been discussed in a previous chapter. Substantial protection can be given to wall panel joints by anticipating the water flow and directing it away from vulnerable areas of the building shell, such as joints. Particular attention should be given to those parts of a wall which experience local build-up of wind pressure (and hence an increased driving-rain index) due to turbulence caused by the shape of the building. At these points of high risk, joints should be eliminated or reduced to an absolute minimum. No joint, for instance, should be less than 200 mm from a corner, and parapets and heads of walls are also danger areas which call for special care.

In the design of joints the following procedure should be followed in order to achieve the most effective and long-lasting seal.

Progressive steps in joint design

1. Identify and quantify the functional requirements of the joint.
2. Analyse the ways in which water will reach the joint.
3. Design the profiles of the wall components so as to protect joints as much as possible from water flow.
4. Predict the expected range of variations in the joint size due to dimensional variations in the components joined together (dimensional variations due either to manufacturing tolerances or to the physical conditions in which the components function).
5. Select a jointing method that will tolerate the predicted range in 4.
6. Ensure that the joint design gives maximum protection to the seal from water and sunlight (ultra-violet radiation can have long-term harmful effects on some sealing compounds and gaskets).
7. Check that the joint design satisfies the requirements of the particular seal selected.
8. Consider any drainage within the joint, particularly at the intersection of joints. It may be necessary to make a three-dimensional model of such an intersection to assure yourself that the system will drain satisfactorily.
9. Take into account the need to inspect, maintain and replace joined components and jointing elements.
10. Specify precisely all requirements which must be met in order to realise an effective design. The specification will embrace materials used, workmanship, and the quality and performance of the finished joint.

These items will now be examined in more detail.

1. Functional requirements

The function of any particular joint depends on its environment and location, and on the functions and properties of the joined components. A joint may be required to fulfil a vast number of functions in addition to merely keeping the water out. The functions which are derived from the character of the joined components are called *transferred functions*. These are expected to be fulfilled by the joint in order to provide performance continuity from component to component. Table 3/8 lists some of the common transferred functions.

However, in addition to meeting these functions, the joint will have to exhibit certain characteristics which are special to the joint itself. Ease of installation, economic cost, ease of dismantling — these represent special characteristics, and are listed in Table 3/8 as *functions of the joint per se*. Not all functions need to be fulfilled by each joint considered and there may well be wide variations in the required performance standard of indivi-

Table 3/8   Transferred functions and special characteristics of a joint (from BRE Current Paper CP 29/70)

Transferred functions	*Functions of joint per se*
to resist damage by man	to resist dismantling
to prevent passage of odours	to require minimal erection skill
to resist damage by birds	to resist differential deflection of joint components
to prevent passage of insects and vermin	to have economic first cost
to avoid plant growth promotion	to have economic depreciation
to prevent passage of plants, leaves, roots, seeds, pollen	to have economic maintenance cost
to resist passage of fire	to have a width with sufficient permissible tolerance to accommodate thermal, moisture and structural movement, vibration and creep, and variation in work size and in position of joined components
to resist passage of heat	
to prevent passage of light	to require minimal erection time
to resist passage of sound	to permit dismantling
to resist passage of air	to have specified minimum life
to resist damage by polluted air	to be specified in relation to a reference plane
to resist passage of water	components to have specified edge profile
to resist passage of water vapour	to exclude snow if performance would be impaired thereby
to prevent condensation	
to resist damage by water or solutions	to resist passage of water by capillarity
to resist damage by freezing	to exclude solid matter that might prevent movement of components

dual functions. In other words, some requirements are more critical than others. It is important to specify the required performance before choosing the most appropriate jointing method. No sealant or method of jointing will provide a 100% satisfaction for every function. Compromise will be necessary. Therefore to assess the relative importance of the various functions is a very real need.

There will be alternative ways of satisfying each function. For instance, the resistance of a joint to damage by man can be satisfied either by placing the joint sealant far back in the joint, or by using a sealant which is not vulnerable, when it may be used farther forward in the joint, or by protecting a vulnerable sealant by a non-vulnerable baffle. Which of the three alternatives is ultimately selected may well be influenced by one of the more significant functions in the hierarchy of functions that will have been established by the designer.

Clearly, weather exclusion is always high in the hierarchy of functions, but other functions should not be overlooked. The functions required of a joint will condition not only the selection of jointing material, but also the shape of the joint and the corresponding edge profiles of the components. This selection process will have to take into account the dimensional requirements dealt with in point 4.

2 & 3. Water access   The aspects of water flow and water access have been discussed earlier, in Chapter 1. To cope with water exclusion problems the designer will need to consider carefully, from basic principles, the various paths by which water will flow over his building's surfaces.

4. Joint size

The size range of a joint will be controlled by a series of factors which have been previously loosely referred to as tolerances. These are either man-made inaccuracies in manufacture and assembly of the components (now referred to as *induced deviations*), or unavoidable dimensional changes in the components due to moisture content changes or thermal fluctuations (now referred to as *inherent deviations*).

For a joint to be effective, its dimensions must lie within the acceptable range limited by the characteristics of the sealant used. For instance, a gunned mastic can be applied only to a joint of a given minimum width; the minimum width is conditioned also by the ability of the mastic to accommodate the expected movement (inherent deviations) of the components to be joined — i.e. the wider the joint, the greater its capacity to accommodate movement. Similarly, the maximum width is conditioned by the danger of slump in the mastic if the manufacturer's recommendations are exceeded. There is also the consideration of excessive cost if the joint is over-wide. Gasket seals or baffles can be seen to require a width of joint that is controlled within certain limits, such as the dimensions of the devices themselves, their engagement in the recesses provided in the components to be sealed, and the necessity, if they are to provide an effective seal, of being subjected to constant compression, however slight.

Having provisionally selected a jointing method based on the decisions in item 1, the designer can check this against the expected inherent deviations of the components and thereby establish the minimal acceptable joint width which will not cause excessive strain in the sealant medium.

The problem now is to establish the range of joint width that will result from the expected induced deviations of the components to be jointed.

Most manufactured components are produced to a stated tolerance of plus or minus a given dimension. As an example, let us consider a component whose ideal size is 900 mm in width. The manufacturing tolerance will be stated, as for instance ± 10 mm. This means that the *majority* of components will come within a range of a few millimetres on either side of 900 mm. As the inaccuracy increases, so the incidence of the inaccuracy decreases; so that a well manufactured component should show a distribution curve as illustrated in Figure 3/18. A less well manufactured component might show a curve more like that in Figure 3/19. Induced deviations should be restricted within *permissible manufacturing deviation* limits (i.e. ± 10 mm in the example above), but it is not impossible that very occasionally components could fall outside these permissible limits. It is interesting to note that only negative permissible deviations are recommended for precast concrete panels in BS Code of Practice CP 297:1972.

The permissible deviation is established by applying a statistical device — a standard deviation — to the distribution curve of inaccuracy, thereby establishing the probability of components falling outside a particular range of dimensions (Figure 3/20). It would be a reasonable assumption that the quoted manufacturing tolerance (in our case ±10 mm) could represent three standard deviations from the mean. Against this can be assessed the likelihood of components falling to the outside edges of the deviation — or beyond it. A study by the BRE of joint width variations on nine existing buildings illustrates this phenomenon (Current Paper CP 10/73).

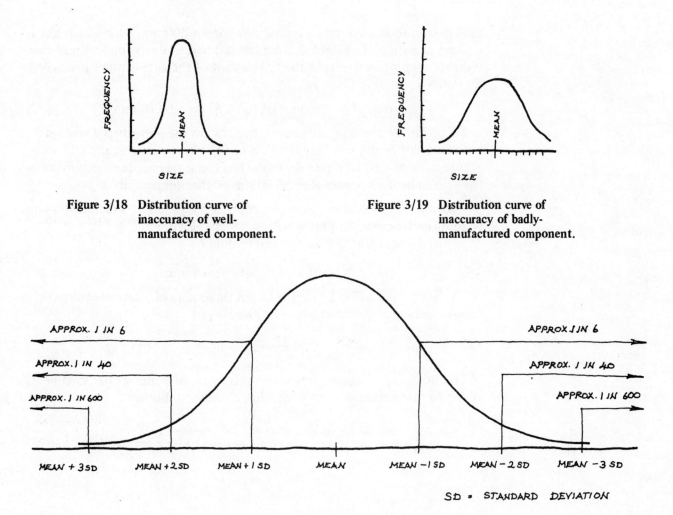

Figure 3/18 Distribution curve of inaccuracy of well-manufactured component.

Figure 3/19 Distribution curve of inaccuracy of badly-manufactured component.

Figure 3/20 Standard deviation applied to distribution curve of inaccuracy.

The problem of anticipating a size range for a joint is based on the probability of inaccuracies either accumulating or cancelling each other out. Referring back to our example, it would obviously be foolish to expect that a series of 900 mm wide components with an induced deviation range of ± 10 mm would all prove to be either 910 or 890 mm wide. There would be a variety of dimensions which, if the components were well manufactured, would contain a greater number towards the mean than towards the outer edges of the permissible range.

If we add the minimum joint width to the width of the largest component, we see that the space into which each of these components would fit would be 910 mm + the minimum joint size. If we were to design for this condition, then the smallest components would be fitting into a space 20 mm greater than that which would be filled by a minimum-sized joint and the joint itself would have to take up the difference, i.e. minimum joint width + 20 mm. This range is clearly too large to be tolerable, but it is, also, based on a faulty use of statistics.

There is a standard statistical method of establishing chance combinations which are likely to occur in practice when a number of random variables are considered. The method involves taking the square root of the sum of the squares of the separate deviations. Suppose, for instance, that our 900 mm component (with a ± 10 mm deviation) is a solid wall panel used in combination with a window component 300 mm wide which has a ± 5 mm deviation. To establish the expected overall deviation of these components in combination take the square root of the sum of the squares of their individual deviations, i.e.

$$\text{overall deviation} = \sqrt{(10^2 + 5^2)} = \pm 11.18 \text{ mm}$$

This figure is a plus or minus deviation, as are the individual deviations; but it is significantly less than the sum of the two deviations, i.e. ± 15 mm. Statistically, the ± 11.18 mm deviation has the same chance of occurring as have the individual permissible deviations of the components.

Taking a more extensive example, suppose two solid wall panels and one window unit were to be placed within a space (Figure 3/21). The overall expected deviation of the components would be

$$\sqrt{(10^2 + 5^2 + 10^2)} = \pm 15 \text{ mm}.$$

The overall deviation divided between three joints (2 joints between components and ½ joint at each end) would give

$$\pm \frac{15}{3} = \pm 5 \text{ mm}.$$

To obtain the designed joint width this figure of 5 mm would then be added to the minimum joint dimension already established.

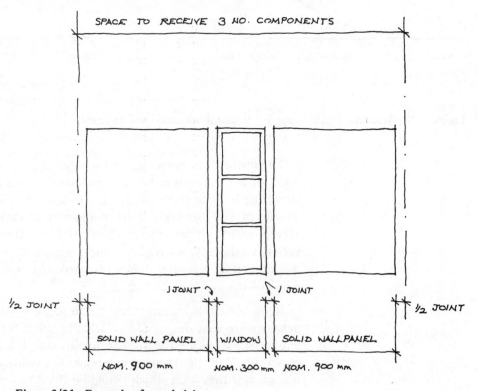

Figure 3/21 Example of panel sizing.

By applying this method, the designer avoids the use of over-large and uneconomic joints. His joint designs are also more likely to be within the dimensional capabilities of the joint sealant finally chosen.

There are, however, types of induced deviation other than manufacturing deviation which can occur in building, and these also affect the joint size.

They are:— setting-out inaccuracies and
positioning inaccuracies of components.

Setting-out inaccuracies can be estimated and assessed, in the light of experience, from the levels of accuracy achieved in other buildings of the same type. Positioning inaccuracies can be totally ignored in the case of small, easily handled components, but can be significant in relation to large precast concrete components.

These inaccuracies must all be accumulated with the component deviation, using the same method as above. The total allowance for deviations (Y) can be obtained from the formula

$$Y = \sqrt{(M_1{}^2 + M_2{}^2 + M_3{}^2 \ ..... + S^2 + P^2)}$$

where M_1, M_2, and M_3 are manufacturing deviations ($\pm$ mm) for the components, S is the deviation in space size caused by setting-out inaccuracies and P is the deviation caused by positioning inaccuracies. Y is a plus or minus value.

The positive value of Y represents the amount by which the whole assembly of components would need reducing in order to fit into the space, making no allowance for even minimum joints. The range of size variation (because Y is a plus or minus quantity) equals 2Y, a dimension which is divided between the number of joints, x.

Therefore the variation in joint size equals 2Y/x or, put another way, disregarding any minimum joint width the range of joint sizes is from 0 to 2Y/x. As 0 mm joints are impractical, this whole range of joint widths must be increased by the width of the minimum joint and the component sizes must be further reduced to provide this required minimum at each joint.

At this point the designer must check whether the initially selected joint sealant is able to perform within the range of widths thus established. Finally the effect of inherent deviations must be taken into account and the amount by which the components will expand must be deduced from their initial size. This last variation in joint width must then be checked with the performance data of the joint sealant.

5 — 8. The selection of a jointing method

As explained at the beginning of this section, joints between wall components are either one-stage joints (filled joints) or two-stage joints (drained joints). As the names suggest the one-stage joint has only one line of defence against the ingress of water, the two-stage joint has at least two lines of defence, maybe more.

Filled joints

Joints shown in Figure 3/22 are developed from a traditional approach to joint design, the earliest form being the mortar joint. However, mortar joints are fundamentally inefficient due to mortars having poor adhesive qualities, being liable to shrinkage and being unable to accommodate movement in the structure or the components. In the past the mortar joint relied on the mass of the structure or on a built-in cavity within the wall to mask its shortcomings, and mortar filled joints are still restricted to traditional applications (mass masonry, brick or block walls, or cavity construction) and to jointing only small components.

Today, filled joints are more often constructed by using sealants or gaskets. Sealants have a greater range of uses than do pure mortars; they have good adhesive qualities and remain flexible, thereby avoiding breakdown

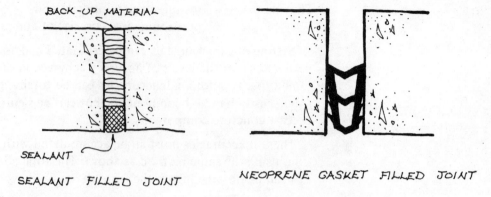

Figure 3/22 Filled joints.

during movement of the components. They are usually applied by gun and can be of the oleoresinous, butyl, acrylic, polysulphide, silicone or polyurethane types. Manufacturers' data should be consulted before a choice of sealant is made. Care must be taken to ensure that the particular sealant will accommodate the joint width range, and also the inherent deviations of the components at the minimum joint width. BS Codes of Practice 297;1972 and 298:1972 set out a table of minimum joint widths of various sealants that will tolerate various extension movements (Table 3/9). Sealants need to be gunned against a back-up material within the joint. This back-up material should be compressible, so that it wholly fills the joint, compatible with the sealant, yet one to which the sealant will not bond. Fibreboard, oil- and bitumen-free rope or expanded plastics can be used with oleoresinous sealants, expanded polyethylene with acrylic, silicone or polyurethane sealants, and expanded rubber or polyethylene with butyl or polysulphide sealants.

Failure of the sealant to adhere to the components or fracture of the sealant will allow air (and therefore water) to infiltrate and, as this is a one-stage joint, failure will ensue. The sealant must never be required to undertake functions in the slightest degree more stringent than those it is guaranteed to perform.

Gaskets (elastic, flexible, or pre-formed extrusions) used in filled joints are placed towards the front of the joint, the shape of the gasket often being produced to suit the internal profile of the joint (Figure 3/23). Gaskets must always be subjected to positive pressure so that they are compressed and deformed to take up the irregularities of the joined components. The surfaces of concrete components are often too rough to allow gaskets to provide effective seals. If the seal is not airtight, the difference in air pressure will force water through the seal. The success of gasket joints depends to a large extent on accuracy in both the manufacture and the

OUTSIDE

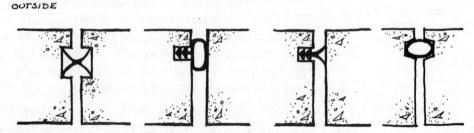

Figure 3/23 Some typical gaskets used in filled joints.

68

Table 3/9 Properties of sealants (derived from information in Table 1, CP 297:1972)

Type	Skinning or setting time (hours)	Max. joint width (mm)	Min. joint depth (mm)	Movement tolerance		Back-up material code
				Butt joint %	Lap joint %	
Oleoresinous						
Knife applied	24	25	13	10–15	25	A
Gun applied	24	13–25	13	10–15	25	B
Butyl						
Knife applied	24	25	7	2–15	5–25	C
Gun applied	24	13–25	7	5–15	10–25	C
Acrylic (solution type)						
Gun applied	24	13–25	7	10–30	25–75	D
Acrylic (emulsion type)	Unsuitable for external joint in UK					
Polysulphide (single part)						
Gun applied	24	13–25	7	15–25	30–60	C
Polysulphide (two part)						
Gun applied	48	25*	7	15–35	30–75	C
Silicones						
Gun applied	2	20	7	15–25	20–30	D
Polyurethanes (single part)						
Gun applied	24	13–25	7	15–30	20–50	D
Polyurethanes (two part)						
Gun applied	24	25*	7	15–35	30–60	D

* wider joints can be filled by build-up techniques   C expanded rubber or polyethylene
A fibre board or rope free from oil or bitumen   D expanded polyethylene
B expanded plastics

assembly of components. Used in one-stage joints, therefore, thye are prone to fail unless the highest standards of workmanship and supervision are maintained.

Drained joints

There are various kinds of drained or open joint. The totally open joint is met with in some cladding applications, where it relies on a completely weathertight backing wall behind, or is used as a rain screen cladding (see Type 3 walling, category (d)). The open drained joint had its origin in Scandinavia in the early '50's. The principle is to remove the jointing medium from the front of the joint. It is thus only applicable where joints are to be made between relatively thick components (e.g. precast concrete wall panels) and where the ingress of water behind the front surface of the component is not harmful to the component (e.g. the case of the timber wall panel with a thin impervious facing is one where drained joints would not be applicable). By removing the jointing medium to a position deep within the joint a drainage channel is formed in the front of the joint which allows the majority of rainwater to fall clear before reaching the medium (Figure 3/24). It has been demonstrated by BRE tests in the Scottish and Plymouth natural exposure rigs that in a plain-sided open joint the majority of rain drains away within the first 50 mm of depth (front to back).

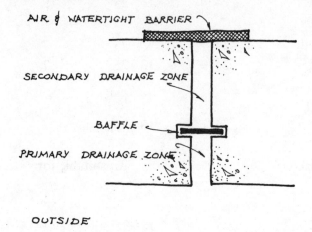

Figure 3/24 Principle of the drained joint.

The effectiveness of the drained joint depends on the efficiency of the airtight and watertight barrier at the back of the joint. If this barrier allows the passage of air, differential air pressure from the front to the back of the joint will carry rainwater across the drainage area. The drainage area in front of the barrier is often divided into two zones by an intermediate baffle. This baffle is usually located in grooves in the edges of the components and can be of aluminium, copper, stainless steel or plastic. The baffle marks the rear of the wetter zone of the drained joint, but both zones should be allowed to drain, as some water in exposed conditions will penetrate beyond the baffle. The profile of the edges of the components may be designed so as to discourage the water driven round the edges of the wall panels from reaching the baffle. BRE test results suggest that an inclined grooving of the edges of wall panels encourages early draining in the joint. A lapped profile, although often troublesome to handle from a design point of view, is certainly most effective in encouraging drainage (Figure 3/25). It

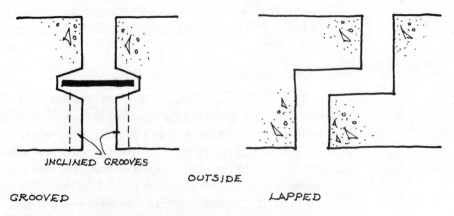

Figure 3/25 Grooved and lapped edge profiles of panels.

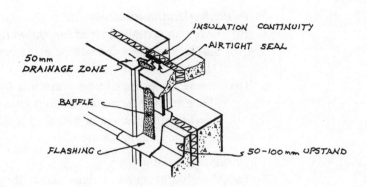

Figure 3/26 Example of a well-designed drained joint (BRE Digest 85).

should be noted that the airtight seal, by being placed at the rear of the joint, should rarely become wet and is also completely protected from ultra-violet radiation and other weathering effects experienced by the sealant in filled joints.

Figure 3/26 shows an example of a joint design that would prove effective in even severe exposure conditions. It demonstrates the chief characteristics of a good drained joint design. These could be summarised as:—

(i) The airtight barrier prevents air infiltration to both horizontal and vertical joints.

(ii) The outer drainage zone (to baffle) measures 50 mm.

(iii) The baffle arrests the progress of wind-driven rain.

(iv) The inner drainage zone clears water penetrating beyond the baffle to a position where it will be directed to the outer face of the building by the flashing in the horizontal joint.

(v) The horizontal joint is protected by a 50 mm (in extreme conditions 100 mm) upstand which must be effectively carried across the intersection with the vertical joints by the flashing.

This design illustrates the principles to be followed. If we now consider the horizontal and vertical joints individually, further points can be emphasised.

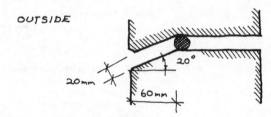

Figure 3/27 Horizontal joint detail (sloping).

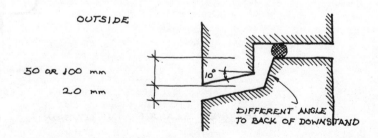

Figure 3/28 Horizontal joint detail (stepped).

In the horizontal joint:—

(a) Given an airtight barrier, an outward slope on both upper and lower surfaces of the joint will be effective in normal exposures (Figure 3/27).

(b) Severe exposure can be overcome by the inclusion of a 50 mm (or a 100 mm in extreme conditions) upstand (Figure 3/28). This expedient should always be resorted to if there is any doubt about the efficiency of the air seal.

In the vertical joint:—

(a) Merely having an airtight seal at the back of the joint reduces water entry into the joint by a third.

(b) Increasing the width of the joint has little effect on the amount of water entering the joint as most of the water flows into the joint round the edges of the components. This should be remembered in designing the components.

(c) Inclined 'wash-board' grooves in the outer zone help to direct the water forward in the cavity (Figure 3/25) and, in fact, when these are used the baffle could be omitted from joints in all but high or very exposed buildings.

(d) Loose baffles and hollow neoprene gaskets provide additional protection. They do not necessarily need to be a tight fit in a correctly designed joint to fulfil this function, and therefore are tolerant of dimensional deviation. However, they should never be relied upon to provide a weathertight seal.

The sealant used in producing the airtight seal should preferably be in rolling shear and not in tension (Figure 3/29). In low buildings backed by in-situ concrete very simple air barriers are possible using a dpc felt held temporarily in position by a gap-filling bituminous adhesive.

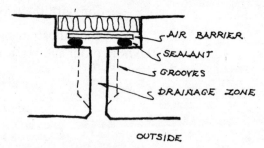

AIR BARRIER SEALANT IN ROLLING SHEAR

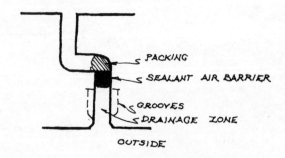

AIR BARRIER SEALANT IN TENSION

Figure 3/29 Air seal in rolling shear and tension, in two types of vertical joint.

Labyrinth joints

Research has been carried out by the BRE into a form of joint in which movements and inaccuracies in component size are less critical and through which the passage of air is not necessarily prohibited. The open drained joint depends for total efficacy on an air seal at the rear of the joint. As air seals invariably rely on some form of sealant, whose life is likely to be less than that of the components joined, the total omission of a seal has obvious long-term benefits.

The joints which the BRE have been examining have labyrinth profiles, the principle of these profiles being that the momentum of the water droplets carried by the airstream into the joint can be used to deposit them in areas of the joint away from the fast airstream, where harmless vertical drainage can take place. Alternatively, penetration can be reduced by design-

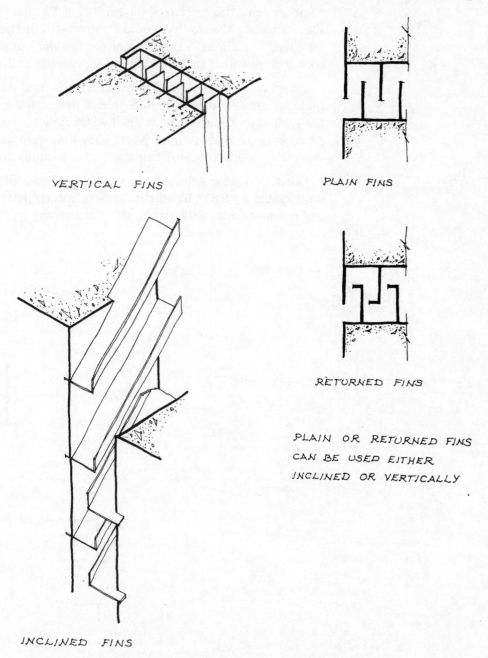

VERTICAL FINS

PLAIN FINS

RETURNED FINS

PLAIN OR RETURNED FINS
CAN BE USED EITHER
INCLINED OR VERTICALLY

INCLINED FINS

Figure 3/30 Diagrammatic illustration of the principles of labyrinth joints.

ing the joint so that the velocity of the air is lowered to a point where it is unable to transport water droplets.

Natural rig tests at Plymouth and laboratory tests have been carried out on a series of vertical joints with labyrinths made up of vertical or inclined fins of various patterns (Figure 3/30). When the joints were left unsealed at the rear, it was found that in the vertical fin labyrinth, water penetrated no farther than the third fin. Sealing the rear of the joint confined the water penetration to the first fin overlap. Varying the amount of fin overlap from 1 mm to 10 mm made no effect on penetration. The test panels were 3 metres high, but it was inferred that these types of joint would perform up to 15 metres in height, provided side-flow into the joint was discouraged by means of ribs or projecting fins on the joined components.

With the inclined fin labyrinths, no water penetrated beyond the first compartment, the overlap of the fins being 10 mm. Observation suggested that increasing the overlap would improve still further the performance of the joint. Variations in the slope of the fins did not seem to affect the performance provided that the slope was greater than 30°.

It can be concluded that labyrinth joints — and particularly the inclined fin labyrinth — provide a high degree of protection to any seal at the rear of the joint and produce a diminished water flow at the intersections as compared with the open drained joint. They have complicated profiles, however, that could prove difficult and costly to apply to claddings.

Horizontal labyrinth joints of varying patterns (Figure 3/31) were also investigated by BRE. Water penetration in each pattern tested was similar and was associated with air velocity through the joint. A critical velocity of

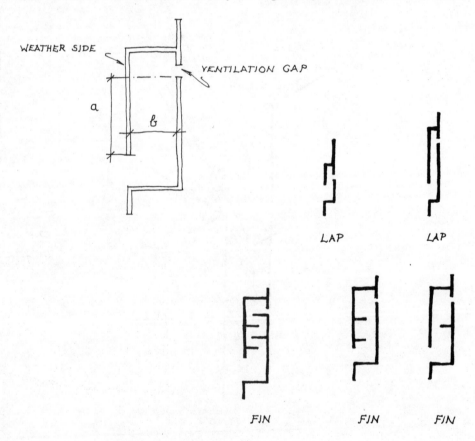

Figure 3/31   Horizontal labyrinth joints.

74

5 m per second appeared to exist, at which speed water droplets would be carried in the airstream. The stages of water penetration are illustrated in Figure 3/32. Further, the weather-side gap of the joint appeared to perform more effectively at 12 mm width than at 6 mm. At the smaller width, droplets of water seemed to form into a 'water plug', which rose between the faces of the joint as the pressure increased. This plug eventually broke to cause penetration. Wind gusting appeared to have little effect until the joint had been penetrated. A simple lap joint (examples marked Lap on Figure 3/31) appeared sensitive to increases in ventilation of the joint, whereas the introduction of overlapping fins (examples marked Fin on Figure 3/31) considerably reduced this sensitivity.

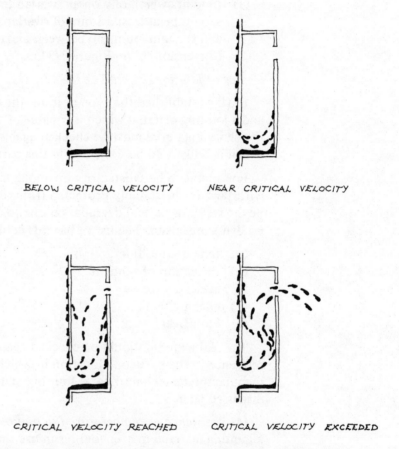

Figure 3/32   Stages in water penetration of horizontal labyrinth joints.

At the time of writing, labyrinth joints have not been produced commercially. A prototype top-hung window employing labyrinth joints has been tested by the BRE and has been proved to prohibit the passage of water at pressure differentials of 80 mm water gauge when opened 2 mm (at a pressure of 25 mm water gauge the window could be opened to 5 mm); but the section profiles are complex and expensive to produce. As yet no commercial use of these principles has been made in wall panel design, although clearly this will eventually occur. Because the labyrinth joint can be designed to accept movement without impairing weather resistance, it is obviously ideal for use in expansion joints, particularly in curtain walling.

The main principles of labyrinth joints can be summarised as follows:—

In both vertical and horizontal joints —
(a)   Ventilation increases the risk of water penetration.

75

(b) An increase in the number of fins reduces this risk at high pressures.

(c) The smallest gap in a joint should be at the back and the gap should not narrow too quickly.

In vertical joints –

(a) In plain fin labyrinths three overlaps are required if the joint is unsealed; one if the joint is sealed. In return fin labyrinths two overlaps are required in an unsealed joint; one in a sealed joint.

(b) Above about 5 mm there is no significant advantage in increasing the overlap.

In horizontal joints –

(a) In joints which rely on an overlap to prevent penetration, there should be at least 13 mm of overlap (dimension 'a' on Figure 3/31) and the minimum gap between meeting faces should be 12 mm (dimension 'b' on Figure 3/31).

Choice of jointing material or seal

Having established the type of joint, the expected range of joint widths and a jointing material which is capable of satisfying these requirements, the chosen material must be checked against a list of natural hazards to which it is likely to be subjected in this particular application.

For a joint to be satisfactory on a long-term basis, its seal must be able to withstand (or be suitably protected from) damage in use. Such damage may be the result of natural degradation due to environmental causes, or attack by living organisms. The list of hazards could be stated as:–

(a) temperature fluctuation

(b) the action of sunlight

(c) attack by ozone

(d) chemical action

(e) biological attack.

The seal material should be checked against each of these hazards with reference to the particular location in which it is used and against the manufacturer's technical data. Jointing materials commonly used will be discussed later.

(a) Resistance to temperature fluctuations. The temperature range which a jointing material may encounter in use can be quite large, particularly in less temperate countries than the UK. The extent of the range can be affected by the colour, finish and location of both the walling elements and the jointing material. It is by no means impossible that a matt black wall panel could experience temperatures ranging from -25° C to +100° C – and these would, to some extent, be passed on to the jointing material both in actual temperatures and in mechanical stresses induced by those temperatures.

Even in the UK wide temperature ranges have been recorded on various materials (Table 3/10).

Table 3/10 Recorded temperatures of various materials (in the UK)

	Max ° C	Min ° C
Light coloured masonry and concrete	50	-20
Dark coloured masonry and concrete	65	-20
Black glass, or metal backed by insulation	80	-25

The seal should, therefore, be capable of withstanding temperatures ranging from -25° C to, say, +90° C. As rubber and plastic materials tend to be affected by heat — softening in the upper range and hardening in the lower — it must be ascertained that the jointing material is still capable of functioning even at the extremes of the range. A mastic sealant should not flow at the higher temperatures, or solidify at the lower; a compression seal or gasket should not soften at the upper end of the range to the extent that it deforms and thereby loses such pressure on the joined components as is necessary to maintain a seal.

Temperature changes can have other effects. Intermittent heating can cause great differential temperature changes between different materials in a wall. The temperature rise in a piece of glass in certain conditions could be as great as 50° C per minute, whereas under similar conditions the temperature rise of an aluminium mullion would only be 10° C per hour. The differential movement so caused will have to be accommodated by the glazing gasket.

The lower end of the temperature range has its own particular problems, for here the jointing material must not freeze, or absorb water, which will freeze. Mastic sealants must not lose adhesion at low temperatures, nor must they solidify, and gaskets whose efficiency depends on their flexibility should not lose that flexibility.

(b) Resistance to the action of sunlight. In the UK the vertical surfaces of a building which face the southern hemisphere, from East to West, will all receive some ultra-violet radiation. Rubbers and plastics can experience attack in the wave length range 290 to 400 mu, but protection can be provided by the inclusion of ultra-violet radiation absorbers or pigments in the compounds. Table 3/11 indicates the long-term test results of exposing some of the less expensive plastic materials to ultra-violet radiation.

Table 3/11   Resistance of plastics to sunlight

Material	*Performance under long-term UV radiation*
PVC	Good if stabilized
Polystyrene	Unsatisfactory
Polyethylene	Good if stabilized or black grade
PF	Slight surface darkening
Rigid polythene	Good if stabilized or black grade
UF	Unaffected
Polypropylene	Satisfactory if stabilized
ABS	Slight yellowing
Polyacetal	Slight chalking
Nylon 6	Slight discolouration

(c) Resistance to attack by ozone. The normal limits of ozone in the atmosphere of the British Isles is between 7 and 12 pp 100 million. The sealing material should resist cracking as a result of ozone attack up to concentration of 16 pp 100 million. BS 903 Part A23 recommends testing in greater concentration.

(d) Resistance to chemical attack. The jointing material should be unaffected by the acids which are present in rain, particularly in heavy industrial areas. Again, some of the less expensive plastics are listed and their resistance to corrosive atmospheres is stated (Table 3/12).

Table 3/12 Resistance of plastics to corrosive atmospheres

Material	Performance when subjected to corrosive atmospheres
PVC	Not affected
Polystyrene	Affected
Polythene	Affected (possible to compound to N/A)
PF	N/A
UF	N/A
Polypropylene	Affected (possible to compound to N/A)
ABS	Affected (possible to compound to N/A)
Polyester	N/A
Polyacetal	N/A
Nylon	Affected

(e) Resistance to biological attack. Such attack can come from fungi, micro-organisms, insects, birds or rodents indigenous to the place of construction. Fungal and bacterial attack are particularly likely to occur in areas with temperatures in the range of 15 to 30° C and with humid conditions.

The design of joints should be such as to impede access by small animals, and the seal materials used should be those not liable to attack in the conditions likely to be encountered.

Table 3/13 gives data applicable to certain plastic materials: —

Table 3/13 Resistance of plastics to biological attack

Material	Termites	Ants, beetles and other insects	Rodents
PVC	No attack	No attack except from German Cockroach	Attacked
Polystyrene	No attack	—	—
Polythene (LD)	10 to 80% destroyed	Slight attack	Attacked
PF	No attack	—	—
Polythene (HD)	Nibbling	Slight attack	Attacked
UF	No attack	—	Attack depends on hardness. When softer than 3 Moh likely to be gnawed
Polypropylene	Nibbling		
ABS	None except with coptotermes and acinaciformus		
Nylons	Slight nibbling	—	—

In addition to the above, man himself provides a hazard to jointing materials, either accidentally (damage by sharp implements — window cleaning gear, lawn mowers, etc.) or wilfully (vandalism). It is always advisable to protect the seal of a vulnerable joint (that is, one within reach of the public) either by placing it deep within the joint or by facing it with a less vulnerable baffle, or by using one of the less vulnerable sealing materials. It must be remembered that man's natural curiosity is expressed in the apparently uncontrollable desire of children of all ages to pick at mastic sealant joints wherever these are noticeable.

9. *The need for maintenance*

The joint design should take into account future maintenance requirements, both for the walling components and for the jointing medium. The actual life expectancy of the components will probably be at least 60 years, unless the building in question is for a short-term purpose. If maintenance work is going to be necessary in order to meet this expectancy, such maintenance work should be considered by the designer, who should feel confident that it will be easy and cheap to carry out. Generally, compression seals or gaskets between heavy wall panels are manufactured of long-term rubbers and are not the cheap, short-life seals used in the motor car industry. They should match the life expectancy of the walling components, since the replacement of such gaskets could be an expensive and difficult operation.

If replacement is envisaged, not only does accessibility need to be assured, but also the financial aspects of replacement must be realistic. Adhesive sealant filled joints, for example, will certainly require replacement during the life of the building. This should be considered in assessing the overall total cost of the jointing system. Initial cost alone is never a fit criterion on which to choose a jointing system.

10. *Specification*

Joints are potentially the area of major risk in any assembly of preformed components. In order to achieve a joint that meets the performance requirements, it is necessary to specify precisely the standards required both in the components and in the joints. These standards should be agreed to be practicable — with the relevant manufacturers — and then clearly defined in terms of materials used, manufacturing standards, workmanship (both in factory and on site), permissible dimensional deviations, methods of site assembly, handling and supervision.

Unless the full process of assembly is visualised and described, it will be impossible to assess, at the time of receiving tenders, whether or not the contractor has appreciated the requirements and realistically priced the operation. To be imprecise will be fair neither to the client, not to the contractor. Further, the designer must be specific about the standards of accuracy required of surrounding structural elements in order to be assured that his calculated joint deviations are achievable.

Joint design summary

Joint efficiency can be achieved only if the designer has considered the following points:—

(1) the way a particular joint will work in practice
(2) initial cost of the joint system
(3) materials used on site
(4) labour required on site
(5) ease of installation and vulnerability to effects of poor workmanship or lack of supervision
(6) skill required for installation
(7) life expectancy of components
(8) maintenance and replacement costs.

If these points are considered in a disciplined fashion, each in turn, first separately then in relation to the other points, and design decisions taken accordingly, an effective system should result. Failures usually occur through the designer's not having analysed the requirements fully and taken steps to achieve them. Joint design cannot be efficient if the thought processes followed are inefficient.

Joint seal materials

This section applies to jointing between both similar and dissimilar wall components or materials.

Seals fall into two categories:–

(a) adhesive seals (mastics), and

(b) compression seals (gaskets).

Adhesive seals

Mastics are marketed either in an unformed state which are gunned or hand applied into joints, or as a roughly pre-formed tape. The unformed material needs skill and experience to apply and can result in high labour costs and levels of wastage which inflate the overall price of the finished job. The use of the tape form reduces both labour costs and wastage.

Adhesive seals are used either in filled joints or to achieve the air-tight seal at the rear of a drained joint. In their unformed state they can also be used for making the seal between different materials in a wall – for instance between brickwork and a door or window frame (Figure 3/15).

The range of these sealants extends from linseed oil and synthetic rubber glazing putties to polysulphide, acrylic, silicone or neoprene based sealants. Generally the performance of polysulphide-based sealants is superior to that of adhesive sealants with other bases for heavyweight wall panel joint applications. These have good ageing characteristics and expansion capabilities, and function satisfactorily over a large range of temperatures. They are, however, relatively expensive. Adhesive sealants based on drying oils and elastomeric polymers are cheaper and are used mainly for minor pointing. Appendix 5 lists a typical selection of proprietary adhesive sealants and their basic characteristics.

Within this section should also be mentioned the self-adhesive foam plastic tapes which are either simple draught exclusion devices (see also Chapter 5) or, in their more heavyweight form, weatherproofing seals. These achieve their effect by the compression of the foam in use. Variation

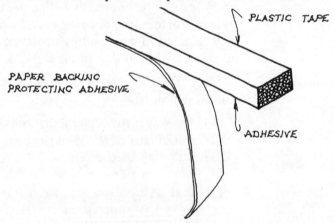

Figure 3/33 Self-adhesive foam plastic tape sealant.

in joint width with these tapes is obviously limited and their use is restricted to relatively minor sealing applications (Figure 3/33). Lightweight tapes used predominantly as draught strips are of open cell foam polyurethane. In addition there are tapes of closed cell foam polyurethane, PVC, synthetic rubber, butyl rubber and polyisobutylene. Appendix 5 includes a few typical proprietary tapes and their recommended uses.

Compression seals   These seals do not depend on the adhesion of the seal to the adjoining components as do adhesive seals. Compression seals, or gaskets, achieve their effect by the fact that they are squeezed between adjoining components and their effort to return to their uncompressed form results in a close contact with the components. Early gaskets were usually of a tubular form. Although these are still used, many authorities claim that greater weather-tightness can be achieved by non-rounded gaskets (fir cone, cruciform or Neofirma type (Table 3/14)). Most gaskets are purpose-made, although some manufacturers over the years have accumulated their designs to provide a standard range. Even when the gaskets are purpose-made, the reasonable cost of the raw materials results in a finished seal which is little more expensive than some of the adhesive sealants.

Gaskets are used not only between similar wall panels in open drained or filled joints, but also as glazing gaskets in windows and curtain walls. Materials used vary from synthetic rubbers to thermoplastics.

Butyl rubber

Butyl rubber is used for inflatable gaskets (EFAB type) (Table 3/14). 'zipper strip' sections (glazing gaskets) (Figure 3/34) and composite gaskets. Butyl is a copolymer of isobutylene and isoprene. It has good resistance to ultra-violet radiation, heat, compression set, tearing, chemicals and vibration, while being impermeable to gases, air and moisture and having low-temperature flexibility. It is capable of 40-50% elongation. A specification for butyl rubbers used for gaskets is contained in BS 4255 Part 1, in which minimum performance figures are given for five classes of hardness:—

Class A	45 ± 5 IRHD hardness
Class B	55 ± 5 IRHD hardness
Class C	65 ± 5 IRHD hardness
Class D	75 ± 5 IRHD hardness
Class E	85 ± 5 IRHD hardness.

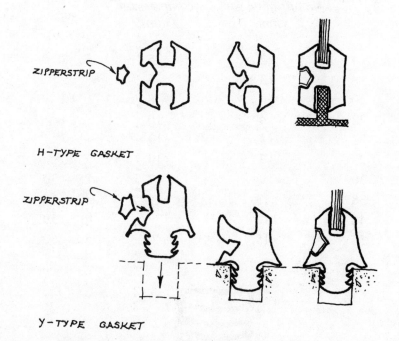

ZIPPERSTRIP

H-TYPE GASKET

ZIPPERSTRIP

Y-TYPE GASKET

Figure 3/34 Zipperstrip in two types of structural gasket.

81

Butyl gaskets operate efficiently at temperatures ranging from -50°C to +150°C. Butyl tapes are effective over a smaller range, -60°C to +70°C.

Neoprene

Neoprene (polychloroprene) is widely used for gaskets in the building industry. The actual grade used is a mercaptan modified polychloroprene rubber with a slow crystallisation rate. Neoprene exhibits a good resistance to water vapour, water, sewage, natural gas, acetic acid, hydrogen sulphide, fuel oil, carbon monoxide, carbon dioxide, ozone and sulphur dioxide. Asphalt, acetone, petroleum oils, lubricating oils and greases have only a moderate effect on neoprene, which is, however, greatly affected by benzene and other aromatic solvents.

Neoprene weathers well, and has fairly good colour retention properties. Black neoprene should be used where light resistance is important. Neoprene gaskets are used both in jointing heavy wall panels and in glazing. Standards of material quality are laid down in the UK by BS 4255: Part 1, 1967 and in the USA by the specifications of the National Association of Architectural Metal Manufacturers (NAAMM). Tensile strengths and characteristics of flexibility and ageing are set out against the hardness classifications (Table 3/15).

Tests for the various properties, set out in ISO, BS and ASTM standards, are shown in Table 3/16.

Table 3/14 Dimensions of typical gaskets

Typical dimensions of Neofirma gaskets (details supplied by Colebrand Limited)

| Width (mm) | Depth (mm) | Total movement in optimum gap (mm) | Max. compression (mm) | Joint movement | | Min. gap depth (mm) |
				Optimum gap (mm)	Max. expansion (mm)	
12	14	±2	5	7	9	20
16	18	±3	6	9	12	25
18	20	±4	8	12	16	25
21	22	±4	10	14	18	30
24	22	±4	13	17	21	30
30	28	±7	13	20	27	35
40	30	±9	17	25 – 30	35	45
50	38	±13	19	30 – 40	45	55
60	48	±13	29	40 – 50	55	65
80	55	±15	40	50 – 60	70	70

NEOFIRMA GASKET

Table 3/14 Continued

Typical dimensions of cruciform gaskets (details supplied by Miles Redfern Construction Services)

Sizes (mm)	Clearance distance (mm)	Max. seal (between faces of contact) (mm)
44.5 × 44.5	63.5	33.3
38.1 × 57.2	57.2	28.6
31.8 × 31.8	47.6	23.8
28.6 × 28.6	44.5	20.6
22.2 × 28.6	44.5	15.9 – 20.6
19.1 × 25.4	38.1	14.3 – 19.1

Typical dimensions of EFAB gaskets (details supplied by Miles Redfern Construction Services)

External diameter (mm)	Internal diameter (mm)	Wall thickness (mm)	Max. gap (mm)	Min. gap (mm)
10.0	7.2	1.40	8.0	3.9
12.5	9.0	1.75	10.0	4.8
15.0	10.8	2.10	12.0	5.8
20.0	14.4	2.80	16.0	7.7
25.0	18.0	3.50	20.0	9.6
30.0	21.6	4.20	24.0	11.5
35.0	25.2	4.90	28.0	13.5
40.0	28.8	5.60	32.0	15.4
45.0	32.4	6.30	36.0	17.3
50.0	36.0	7.00	40.0	19.2
55.0	39.6	7.70	44.0	21.2

EFAB GASKET

STAGE 1.
GASKET RELAXED

STAGE 2.
EVACUATED SEAL READY FOR INSERTION

STAGE 3.
GASKET PLACED & VACUUM RELEASED

Table 3/15 Neoprene strengths and flexibility. Comparison of UK and USA Standard requirements.

	B.S. 4255 Hardness ± 5 IRHD					NAAMM specification Hardness ± 5 IRHD				
	A	B	C	D	E					
Before ageing	46	55	65	75	85	40	50	60	70	80
Tensile strength Kgf/cm²	150	120	140	125	120	112	112	112	127	127
Elongation at break	450	300	250	180	100	450	300	250	200	180
% Compression set % @ 70° C	25	25	25	25	25	30	30	25	25	25
After ageing	72 hours @ 100° C					70 hours @ 100° C				
Tensile strength % of unaged value	85	85	85	85	85	85	85	85	85	85
Elongation at break % of unaged value	60	60	60	60	60	60	60	60	60	60
Hardness change IRHD	+10 - 0	+10	+10	+10	+10	+15 - 0	+15 - 0	+15 - 0	+15 - 0	+15 - 0
Stiffening at low temperatures 7 days @ -10° C ±1° C	Difference in hardness max. 12 IRHD					Low temperature brittleness no visible cracking @ - 45° F				
Ozone resistance	–					1 ppm ozone for 500 hours @ 20% elongation – no cracking				
Dimensional stability	–					1" x 2" x 0.080 strip aged as above – max. change in width or length 2%				

Table 3/16 Standard tests for neoprene

Properties of neoprene	Relative standards		
	ISO	*BS*	*ASTM*
Hardness	R 48 – 1947	903,A26	Shore Duro A 676
Tensile strength	R 37 – 1957	903,A2	D 412
Compression set	R 37 – 1957	903,A6	D 395
Heat ageing	R188 – 1961	No equivalent, but 903,A19 similar	D 865
Low temp. brittleness	R188 – 1961	903,A25	D 746
Weather (ozone) resistance	R188 – 1961	903,A23	D 1149

Extrusion accuracy has been a problem with neoprene, but as experience has increased, so the problems have been resolved.

Cellular neoprene is sometimes used. It is very resilient, and can be given additional weather resistance by a coating of chlorosulphorated polyethylene.

Used as glazing gaskets, neoprene allows panels to float in a resilient bed. Installation is easy and is unaffected by the weather. It is also a clean process.

Neoprene gaskets have been used in the USA for over 25 years and accelerated weathering tests have shown a life expectancy of over fifty years.

Other rubbers

Other rubbers are specified in BS 4255 including chlorobutyl and ethylene propylene terpolymers. The standard gives ample data.

Costs of seals

Costs of seals must be assessed in terms of their overall installed costs and expected life span, taking into account maintenance or replacement costs.

Neoprene is only 20% more expensive than good adhesive seals, but saves 50-56% of installation costs of a polysulphide seal and gives at least a 50 years' life. Butyl, either as a gasket or a sealant, is about 50-90% more expensive than oil putty, but the latter has a life of only 5 to 10 years.

Glazing gaskets can be substantially more expensive than putty, but putty would certainly fail under conditions which will easily be overcome by gaskets.

Glazed elements

Glazed elements may serve either a dual purpose — that of providing ventilation as well as illumination to the building interior (openable windows), or a single purpose — that of illumination only (fixed glazed panels). Both types of glazed element can be combined (a glazed component of more than one panel, some openable, some not). After the introduction of curtain walling, the practice of 'glazing' with non-transparent materials became a normal part of building, such solid (or infill) panels being incorporated into the curtain wall skeleton of mullions and transoms in those areas where light and ventilation were not required (i.e. the floor/ceiling zone of the elevation). Their method of installation (and consequently their potential failure) is similar to that of the glass areas of the curtain wall.

Leakage of air and water can occur either at the junction between exterior frame and opening light frame (frame-to-frame failure) or between glass and frame (glass-line failure). It is interesting to note that in both the BS 4315 and the Agrément tests there is an assumption that fixed lights do not leak — a patently inaccurate belief — and consequently air leakage is related to area of opening light or length of meeting frame around the opening light. It is only when BS 4315 considers gasket glazing systems that the possibility of leakage in fixed glazing is accepted. In practice, however, leakage does occur at the glass-to-frame line both in the putty glazed domestic timber window and the more sophisticated sealant glazed windows.

Frame-to-frame draught and weather stripping

Draught and weather stripping associated with glazed elements will be dealt with in Chapter 5, where minor weatherproofing and remedial operations are considered. Often the use of draught proofing devices is an admission of failure, or a late effort to make earlier design details live up to expectations. It should, however, be realised that in most high performance windows and doors the necessary devices are already in-built. Far from being an admission of design inadequacies, this shows a realisation of the fact that in order to meet high performance requirements (as detailed in Chapter 2) a window or door will need such devices.

Glazing methods

Apart from the actual design of the window frame, which can lead to failure to keep out air and water, the other point of possible failure in a window occurs at the glass-to-frame joint. This joint can, on the one hand, be a very simple putty joint of relatively short life or, on the other hand, be the principal risk area in a curtain wall.

One of the causes of faulty joints at the glass line is the use of an unsatisfactory glazing method. BS Code of Practice 152:1972, Glazing and Fixing of Glass for Building, deals with Group 1 materials (linseed oil and metal casement putty) and Group 2 materials (non-setting compounds for use with beads) and the Code should be consulted regarding details of glazing techniques.

The correct detailing of the glazing rebate is essential if glass-line failure is to be avoided. The depth of the rebate should allow for the necessary edge clearance of the glass and the minimum edge cover (Figure 3/35). Edge cover varies with the size of glass. Up to 1.5 m² glass size the edge cover should be 9 mm, from 1.5 m² to 3.5 m², 12 mm, and above that size a specialist should be consulted. Edge clearance for normal glass should be 3 mm; for double glazed units where the unit thickness is 16 to 25 mm, or the unit area is 3.0 m² to 8.5 m², edge clearance should be increased to 5 mm; for heat absorbing and coloured glass where the larger dimension exceeds 750 mm, edge clearance should be similarly increased to 5 mm. Glass should be set in the aperture with setting blocks at the cill and location blocks at the jamb and head to give even clearance to all edges. Blocks should be of resilient, non-absorbent material (PVC, rigid nylon, etc.) (Figure 3/36). Distance pieces should be used to prevent displacement of glazing compound under wind pressure. These should be 25 mm long and

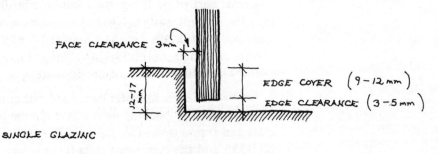

SINGLE GLAZING

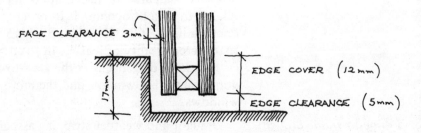

DOUBLE GLAZING WITH SEALED UNITS

Figure 3/35 Glazing rebate sizes.

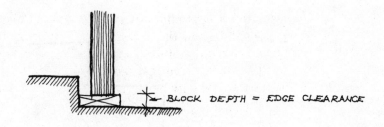

SETTING & LOCATION BLOCKS

BLOCK DEPTH = EDGE CLEARANCE

BLOCK DEPTH = FACE CLEARANCE

NB: POSITIONS OF SETTING BLOCKS & DISTANCE PIECES MUST NOT COINCIDE

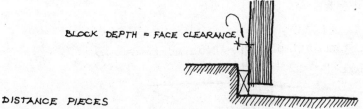

DISTANCE PIECES

Figure 3/36 Setting blocks and distance pieces for glazing.

their depth should be such as to allow them to be covered by at least 3 mm of compound.

Putty and sealant glazing

The simplest form of glazing is so-called face glazing (Figure 3/37); i.e. glazing not involving the use of a bead. Face glazing should be restricted to low or medium rise applications, small panes of glass and areas of only moderate exposure. The glazing medium is either linseed oil putty or metal casement putty depending on the type of frame. Putties are designed to harden fairly rapidly and must be painted regularly to encourage the retention of any degree of flexibility. Glass should be solidly bedded with putty, including back putty, between the glass and the rebate face.

Bead glazing covers a wide range of glazing types from the small to the large and sophisticated. At the smaller end of the range the glass is solidly bedded in a hand-grade compound — usually referred to as a non-setting compound (Figure 3/38). This is a misleading name as, although the material forms a skin which slows down the 'through' hardening process, these compounds do eventually set. They are usually oil-based, with synthetic polymers included to improve flexibility and lengthen the life. Often they are referred to as butyl or butyl-enriched compounds. Painting is not necessary, but it does help to improve the compound's life. Hand-grade compounds have a normal life expectancy of 5 to 10 years, but if they are subjected to abnormal demands — if they are used for very large panes of glass, double glazed units, or solar control glass — this life could be considerably reduced. Hand-grade compounds should be used for relatively small pane glazing of an undemanding nature. For more demanding applications a glazing sealant should be used.

A sealant cures chemically after application and is usually based on acrylic terpolymers or polysulphides. It has a long life (possibly in excess of 20 years) and will tolerate severe movement and exposure. The material is relatively expensive and solid bedding in sealant (Figure 3/39), while being completely effective for larger glazing applications, is costly both in labour and materials.

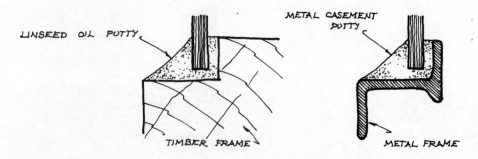

Figure 3/37 Face glazing.

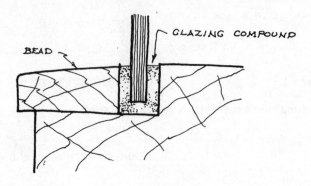

Figure 3/38 Bead glazing.

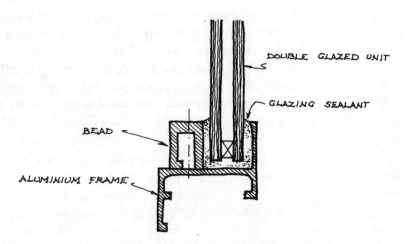

Figure 3/39 Solid bedded glazing in sealant (normal UK method).

The use of pre-formed tapes (strip compounds) in conjunction with sealant, overcomes some of the cost objections of solid bedding in sealant by reducing labour costs (Figure 3/40). Pre-formed tapes, commonly referred to as 'load-bearing' (not a strictly accurate description), are either oil-based or of a synthetic rubber polymer formulation. The 'load-bearing' properties of the particular tape must be ascertained and care taken to work within this limitation, unless additional support to the glazing is provided. Pre-shimmed tape — a tape with a true load-bearing capacity due to the incorporation of a rubber rod in the tape as a distance piece — is available and this avoids the use of independent distance pieces which are often necessary with ordinary pre-formed tapes. The tape is usually capped externally with a sealant. It is important that the space allowed for the sealant is sufficient, otherwise the tape tends to force itself through the sealant. The application of the capping requires considerable skill.

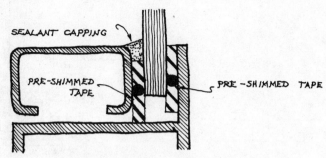

Figure 3/40 Glazing with preformed tape.

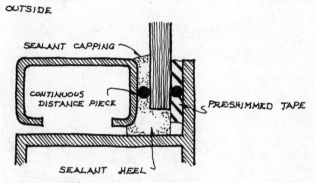

Figure 3/41 Outside beading with tape.

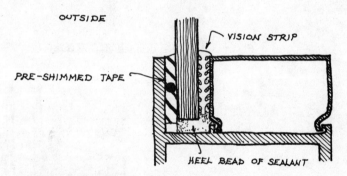

Figure 3/42 Inside bead glazing with vision strip.

A combination of pre-formed tape and sealant is particularly suited to outside bead glazing (Figure 3/41). The sealant is applied in two operations – the first as a heel bead, the second as a capping over a continuous distance piece. An alternative system (Figure 3/42) employs a neoprene or PVC vision strip. This is designed especially for inside bead glazing. The strip, when forced down into the sealant heel bead, induces compression in the whole glazing system.

Drained glazing

Drained glazing techniques have become the subject of considerable development activity in recent years. It has been found that even solid bedded glazing in high quality sealant allows water to penetrate into the glazing rebate, where it is trapped. Hermetically sealed double glazed units in these conditions will suffer deterioration. The principle of drained glazing is that the glass is sealed to the rebate and the frame is designed to drain water from under the glass, either through the outside bead or the frame.

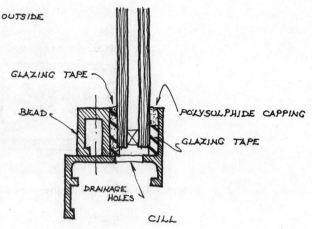

Figure 3/43 Normal Continental glazing method.

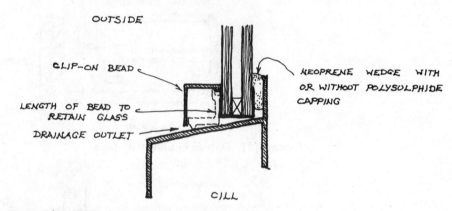

Figure 3/44 BRE drained glazing system.

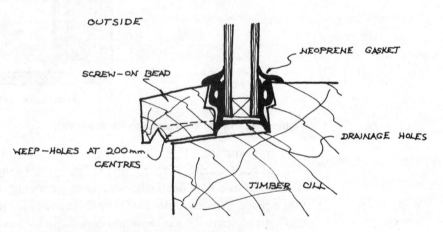

Figure 3/45 Knag drained glazing system.

The use of drained glazing techniques with double glazed sealed units appears preferable to other glazing techniques and this has led to recent research by BRE (CP 56/74) where the amount of water penetrating a series of glazing joints was examined. The solid bedded joint in the test series not only leaked, but retained the water much longer in the glazing rebate than did the continental detail (Figure 3/43), which allows water to drain through the frame. This typical continental joint, however, did not achieve results equalling those of the BRE drained system (Figure 3/44), or the Norwegian Knag gasket system (Figure 3/45). The latter is an interesting example of a drained gasket which appears to be very successful.

From the BRE's work the following recommendations emerged:—

(a) drainage through the frame must be handled with care to avoid the discharge from the drainage holes damaging or defacing the surrounding structure;

(b) systems (such as the Knag system) when used with timber frames must employ preserved timber and beads that are not vulnerable to rot;

(c) dry glazing systems are recommended for use with hermetically sealed double glazing units;

(d) drained systems are not vulnerable to conditions of severe exposure.

Glazing direct into concrete panels has become a more common feature following the increased use of air conditioning. Figure 3/46 illustrates a method employing tape, sealant and neoprene or PVC vision strips.

Gasket glazing

All glazing systems mentioned so far (with the exception of the Knag system) have been sealant systems. The other method of dealing with major glazing is the use of neoprene gaskets — either structural or non-structural. Neoprene, as a material, has been discussed at length earlier in this section.

Non-structural gaskets are normally 'U' shaped. They snap around the outer edge of the glass and are squeezed into position by the glazing bead. The system relies entirely on the pressure applied by the bead to produce a watertight seal (Figure 3/47).

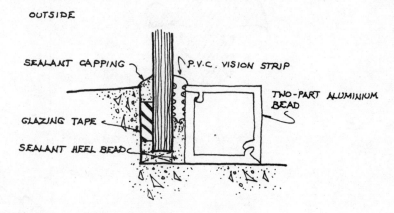

Figure 3/46 Glazing direct to concrete.

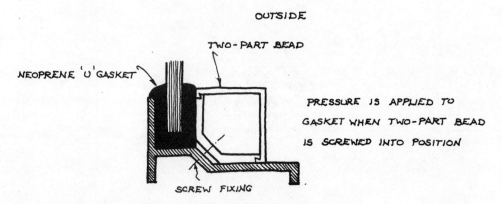

Figure 3/47 'U' shaped glazing gasket (non-structural).

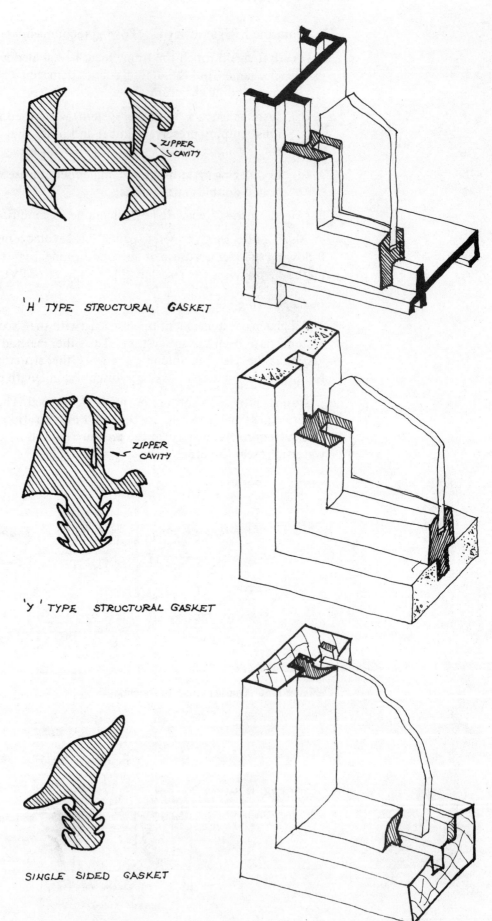

'H' TYPE STRUCTURAL GASKET

'Y' TYPE STRUCTURAL GASKET

SINGLE SIDED GASKET

ZIPPER CAVITY

ZIPPER CAVITY

Figure 3/48 Structural gaskets.

Structural gaskets rely on the fundamental property of rubber – that it cannot be compressed, only displaced. Structural gaskets are either 'H', 'Y' or single-sided type. The first two incorporate a separate insert or 'zipper-strip' of hard rubber which applies a continuous pressure to the assembly (Figure 3/48). Corner sections are factory moulded and all three types can be amalgamated into horizontal or vertical ladder gaskets with factory moulded T junctions. In ladder gaskets, the mullions or transoms are not in themselves strong enough to withstand wind loads. The strength of the installation comes from the strength of the infill and the span of the ladder is clearly a significant factor in the strength of the assembly. Vertical ladder gaskets with unsupported horizontal members (transoms) can be used up to a maximum height of 6 metres. Glass thickness and maximum span should be discussed with the gasket manufacturer. The ladder gasket is a half-way stage between the window and the curtain wall.

As previously mentioned, gasket glazing systems were the subject of a special test in BS 4315 (Part 1, Test C). This test is designed to simulate

1. Clear Glass housed in 'H' type or 'Grooved' type gaskets. Three second Mean Wind loading. Four edge support.

2. Clear Glass—glazed with Miles Redfern 'Presslock' type gasket. Three second Mean Wind loading. Four edge support.

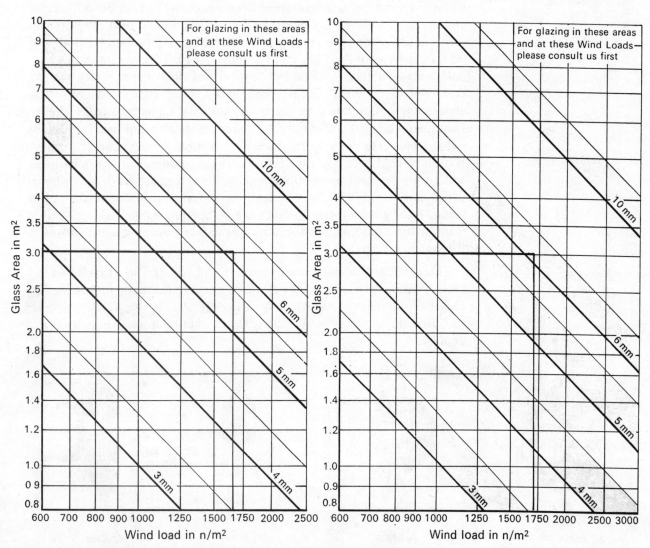

Figure 3/49 Gasket glazing graphs (Miles Redfern Construction Services).

gusting wind and by imposing cyclic pressures reproduces the pumping action that could force water through gasket systems. Most manufacturers of gaskets maintain their own consistent testing programme and claim impressive results.

The thickness of glass is important in the satisfactory operation of gasket systems, since it affects the amount of deflection of glass under pressure. One manufacturer gives guidance on this aspect in the form of two graphs (Figure 3/49). The thick base line of each toned zone is for use when the ratio of long to short sides of pane is 1:1; the extreme of the toned zone is when the ratio is 3:1. Interpolations can be made between 1:1 and 3:1. Where the ratio exceeds 3:1, the gasket manufacturer should be consulted. Given a glass area of 3.00 m² it will be seen from the graphs that 'H' or 'Y' type gaskets with 6 mm thick glass can withstand a 3 second mean wind load of 1650 N/m². For the single-sided gasket, however, the capability is 1700 N/m².

This type of installation should be discussed with the gasket manufacturer at design stage.

Curtain walling

Neoprene structural gaskets have made a significant impact on curtain wall design. They are commonly used in the H or Y form to lock glass to metal mullions and transoms, providing a resilient bed for both the glass and the sheet infill alike (Figure 3/50), but the most recent development is for their use in an external facade which has no exposed metal at all — only infill (usually glass) and neoprene (Figure 3/51). This system avoids the cold bridge which is so often the down-fall of the cheaper metal box section curtain walling system. The neoprene faced system arrives on site with each aluminium section fitted on the front face with a length of gasket 3% longer than the metal, but compressed to about 6% shorter and held in place by nylon bands. The walling framework is assembled and a neoprene cruciform section is fixed over the intersections. The restraining bands are then cut and during the next few hours the neoprene returns to its original shape which, because it is 3% too big, forms a compression seal with the cruciforms. Ideally this system should have no opening lights, although one manufacturer has now produced neoprene-faced opening lights for use with the system.

This is a sophisticated type of curtain wall and care must be taken in its design, ensuring that too large sheets of glass are not hung on too small gaskets. Compliance with the American draft ASTM specification C 542/65T is essential, and consultation with the manufacturer is equally important.

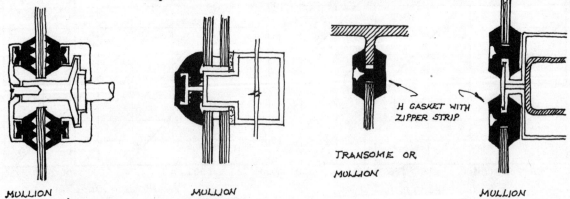

MULLION   MULLION   TRANSOME OR MULLION   MULLION

H GASKET WITH ZIPPER STRIP

Figure 3/50 Neoprene gaskets in curtain walling.

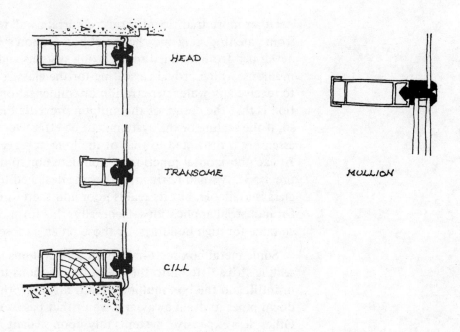

Figure 3/51 Totally neoprene-faced curtain walling.

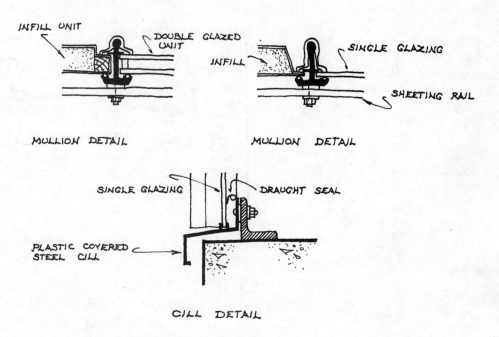

Figure 3/52 Patent glazing curtain wall details.

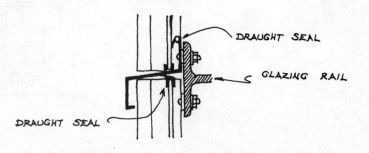

Figure 3/53 Horizontal flashing in vertical patent glazing.

Other more traditional forms of curtain wall include those developed from patent glazing and the metal box section systems. The former has been developed from inclined roof glazing systems and is a simple assembly of mullions, which provide a seating for the glass, a double seal and a channel to receive any water penetration or condensation (Figure 3/52). Its limitation is that the design of the mullion prevents the introduction of a transom so, if the sealing of the system is to be effective, the maximum depth of the assembly is restricted to that of the longest piece of glass or infill available. At each horizontal junction, a complete horizontal flashing is required (Figure 3/53). A small horizontal flashing designed to fit between sheets of glass is available, but its seal is poor and therefore its use should be reserved for industrial applications. Generally, this form of curtain walling is not suitable for high buildings, or those on an exposed site.

Some metal box section curtain wall systems have sophisticated neoprene sealing strips fitted into the metal box sections to provide the seal to glass or infill, and the box mullions and transoms form a system of gutters and down pipes to drain away any water that passes the outer seal (Figure 3/54). Other, less expensive, systems rely upon sealant joints between the glass and the lugs on the sides of the mullions and transoms (Figure 3/55). Great care is necessary in aligning this type of system if it is not to leak, and the skill

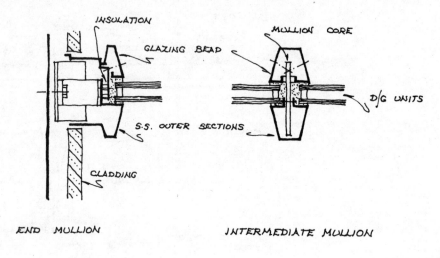

END MULLION   INTERMEDIATE MULLION

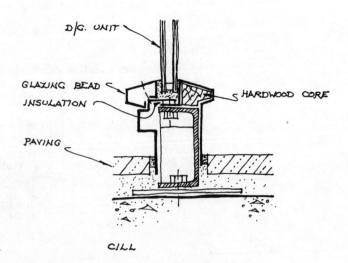

CILL

Figure 3/54 High quality metal box section curtain walling.

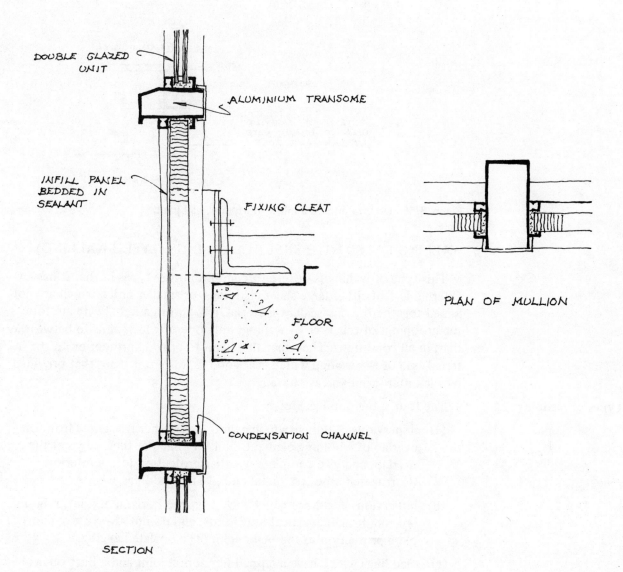

DOUBLE GLAZED UNIT

ALUMINIUM TRANSOME

INFILL PANEL BEDDED IN SEALANT

FIXING CLEAT

FLOOR

CONDENSATION CHANNEL

SECTION

PLAN OF MULLION

Figure 3/55   Simple aluminium box section curtain walling.

in placing the sealant is of paramount importance. Cold bridging through the mullions and transoms can lead to condensation problems. The more expensive systems avoid this by breaking the continuity of the metal box, whilst other systems contain channels to collect condensation and possible leakage and convey it harmlessly outside the building.

For exposed conditions the designer would be well advised to consider carefully before deciding to use the cheaper versions of the metal box section type of curtain wall. Economy at this stage can lead to later maintenance problems that could prove very expensive indeed.

Drained joint between glazed and solid elements

It is possible to apply the BRE open drained joint principles to the junction between major glazed elements and solid wall panels, when both have sufficient depth. Figure 3/56 illustrates a typical application. The air seal appears, as in the previous examples, at the rear. A baffle discourages rain blowing straight into the drainage area. Water penetrating the drainage area is allowed to drain harmlessly down on to an extended cill and, from there, is directed outside the building.

97

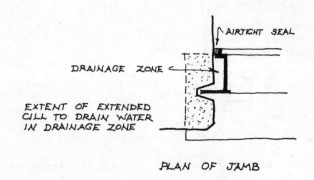

PLAN OF JAMB

Figure 3/56 Drained joint as applied to window/wall joint.

WALLING FACED WITH SHEET CLADDINGS (TYPE 3 WALLING)

This type of walling is different from both other types in that it has an external leaf of either large sheet claddings, or smaller units, which are not joined together by any sealant material, mortar or gasket. There are four sub-groupings of this type of walling, only one of which aims to be weather-tight in all conditions. The other three aim to provide protection to the internal skin of the walling which is as good as, or better than, that provided by the outer skin of a cavity wall.

Types of cladding

The four sub-groupings are: —

(a) impervious claddings which gain their weather resistance from the overlap of adjoining elements and the shape of their edges at the overlap, and give complete weather protection to the interior. (Corrugated asbestos, metal and plastic claddings.)

(b) impervious claddings which have a lapped horizontal joint, rely on layered, broken, vertical butt joints, and do not always give complete protection to the inner skin. (Tile or slate hanging.)

(c) claddings which have a lapped horizontal joint and a butt vertical joint and do not give complete protection to permeable inner skins. (Asbestos shingles, flat asbestos sheets, weather-boarding of timber, asbestos or PVC, asbestos or timber siding.)

(d) impervious claddings which have open joints (both horizontal and vertical, rely on the geometry of the joint to discourage ingress of water, and require intermittent or continuous protection to the inner skin to prevent excessive dampness. These are known as rain screen claddings.

(a) Fully overlapping claddings

This category of walling is one in which the inner skin of the wall will remain fully protected and therefore can be made of moisture sensitive or permeable materials. The external skin consists of large sheets of material such as corrugated asbestos or metal. The cladding depends for its effectiveness on the overlap at the vertical and horizontal joints and on the profile at the vertical edge of the sheets which prevents water from driving up between the sheets. Flashing pieces are produced, of matching profile, to close the claddings at head, cill and jambs and make connection with glazing and door frames. The exact details vary with the profile and the type of cladding, but Figure 3/57 illustrates a few typical details.

This form of walling, most commonly used in industrial buildings, is attached directly to steel frames. In order to avoid further operations of

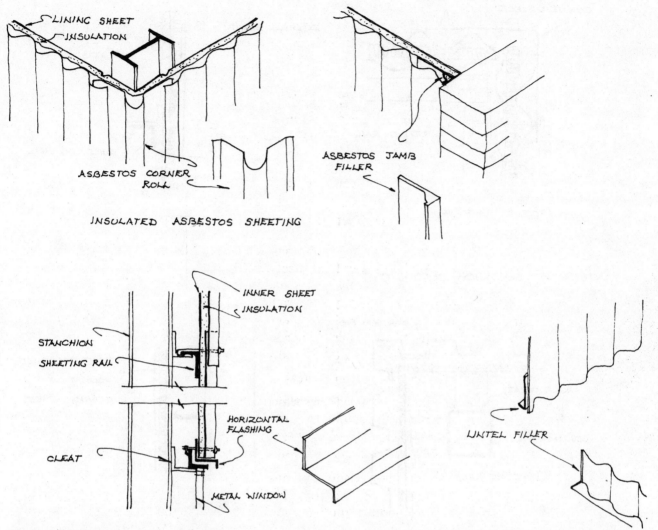

LINING SHEET
INSULATION

ASBESTOS CORNER ROLL

INSULATED ASBESTOS SHEETING

ASBESTOS JAMB FILLER

INNER SHEET
INSULATION

STANCHION

SHEETING RAIL

CLEAT

HORIZONTAL FLASHING

METAL WINDOW

LINTEL FILLER

Figure 3/57 Typical large sheet claddings.

forming the internal lining and installing the insulation, sandwich cladding systems have been developed which provide external cladding, insulation and lining in one operation (Figure 3/58).

Because this form of walling is usually through-fixed, the fixing positions become points of possible leakage. Consequently, a wide range of weather-protected heads and washers is available for use with the fixing devices in order to maintain the weathertight integrity of the walling (Figure 3/59). Thus these large sheet materials can provide a simple watertight shell if the manufacturer's advice is followed and if the sheeting is not damaged during or after installation.

Also in this category, but not providing complete weathertightness, are some vinyl and aluminium claddings in smaller widths (usually 300 mm) and with vertical interlocking edge profiles (Figure 3/60). These claddings, while intended to protect the backing wall, will be penetrated by rain in extreme conditions. To guard against this, the backing wall should be protected by roofing felt, building paper or polythene sheeting; or alternatively should itself be impermeable.

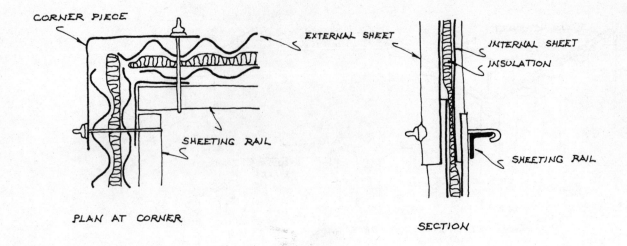

PLAN AT CORNER

SECTION

ASBESTOS SANDWICH CLADDING

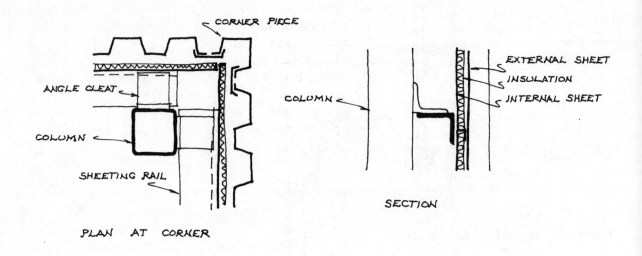

PLAN AT CORNER

SECTION

STEEL SANDWICH CLADDING

Figure 3/58 Sandwich claddings.

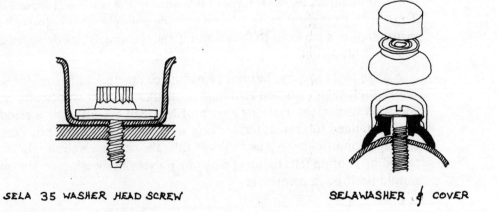

SELA 35 WASHER HEAD SCREW

SELAWASHER & COVER

Figure 3/59 Weather protected heads and washers.

100

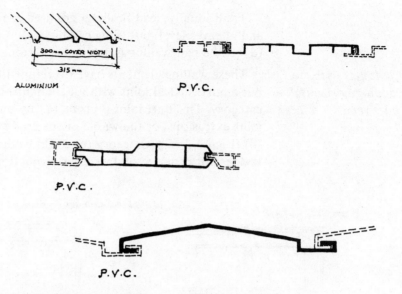

Figure 3/60 Some narrow aluminium and PVC claddings.

(b) Claddings with overlapping horizontal and layered butt vertical joints

This category consists of small cladding elements with butt vertical joints, fixed in several layers with neighbouring layers breaking joint. The horizontal joint is an overlap (Figure 3/61). Generally this category of walling (including tile and slate hanging) will resist driving rain in all but the most extreme conditions. Because of this danger of penetration under certain conditions, it is recommended that the backing wall should be protected by polythene sheeting, building paper or roofing felt; alternatively, the backing wall itself should be impermeable.

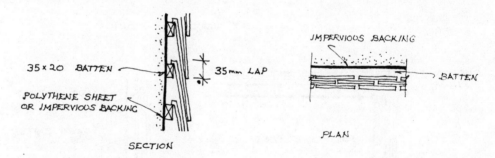

Figure 3/61 Tile or slate hanging.

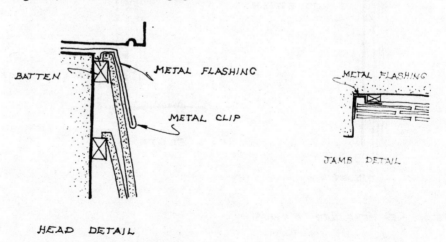

Figure 3/62 Lead flashings to tile hanging.

101

Traditionally, lead flashings are used around all openings (Figure 3/62) and at eaves level, but tiling can be used as an open joint cladding (Group (d)) if the rear walling is detailed accordingly.

(c) Claddings with overlapping horizontal and butt vertical joints

These walling elements have overlapped horizontal joints (as Group (b)) but a butt vertical joint without the multi-layer arrangement of the previous category. This butt joint is protected by bituminous felt strips or aluminium joint extrusions, or the whole of the rear walling is protected as in category (b) (Figure 3/63). Category (c) could be designated semi-open joint cladding. It does not provide total weather-protection to the rear walling.

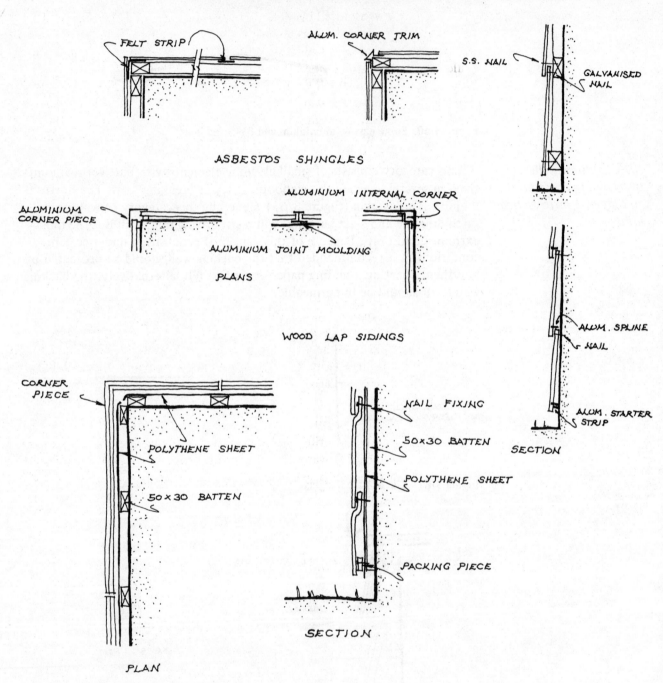

Figure 3/63 Claddings with overlapping horizontal and butt vertical joints – typical details.

(d) Open joint rain screen claddings

In this form of wall, it is assumed that air and water will penetrate the joints in the outer skin of the wall. Jointing, therefore, is very simple and an effort is made to drain away as quickly as possible all the water which passes into the cavity behind the rain-screen cladding so that it will not reach the inner skin in sufficient quantities to cause damage. The rain screen skin is used to protect the inner part of the wall from the majority of driving rain (being, in this respect, similar to tile hanging and cavity construction), but taking advantage of thin — often large — sheet materials, or thin slab materials (natural stone). Such thin materials would be difficult and expensive to seal satisfactorily. In cold climates this form of construction, by providing thermal insulation at the outer face of the wall, enables intersticial condensation to be avoided. By opening the bottom of the cavity to the outside air, the air pressure in the cavity and that outside the building shell tend to equalise, thereby largely preventing the build-up of differential pressure which would drive water through the joints. It seems advisable to seal cavities at the corners as wind can produce large pressure differences between adjacent sides of a building. Over-ventilation of the cavity will result in a loss of the thermal insulation that would otherwise be given to the wall.

The Norwegian Building Research Station have carried out considerable work on open joint walling of asbestos cement sheets, thin timber and stone slabs. The BRE has recently taken up this research (CP 89/74). It has monitored rain penetration into joints between 6 mm and 64 mm thick cladding panels. It was found that water penetrates the rain screen in two ways: (a) it crosses the cavity, or (b) it runs down the back of the rain screen. The amount of water reaching the rear walling varied only according to the width of the joint. In other words, the rain crossing the cavity was approximately equal to the amount of driving rain on the area of the joint. It was, however, scattered on the rear wall in a fan pattern (Figure 3/64). If the joints could be dimensionally restricted to 2.5 mm (vertical) and 5 mm (horizontal), little water would cross a cavity with a minimum depth of 25 mm. This discipline, however, is too rigorous, particularly for thicker claddings. It might be more practical to apply the restriction to horizontal joints only, while screening the vertical joints by felt strips (Figure 3/65).

Most of the water entering the joint ran down the back of the rain screen, and most of this water was the result of side-flow from the adjacent faces of the cladding. Corrugations on the edge of the panel would reduce this flow. In the case of thicker panels, flow could be reduced by inclined

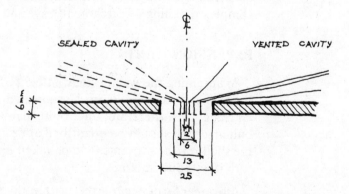

Figure 3/64 Water scatter through open joint (from BRE CP 89/74).

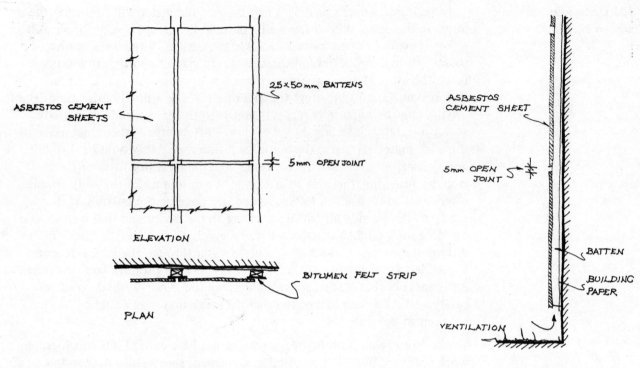

Figure 3/65 Norwegian type of rain screen walling.

grooves in the panel edges (Figure 3/25). With thicker panels, the joint width made little difference to water ingress where the cavity was a sealed one; with unsealed cavities, the smaller the joint the greater the penetration. This pattern was less well defined in the case of thin panels.

In open joint walling the sensitivity of the inner wall to moisture is important in determining the degree of screening necessary behind the open joints. Our experience in this country is still limited and, if the designer is in doubt, the inner leaf should be protected by building paper or felt. Heavier claddings are less accurate in size than thin claddings, with consequent variation in joint size. This can lead to unforeseen degrees of leakage.

Generally this form of walling would seem to be one of considerable attraction and its use is likely to increase. It avoids the use of expensive sealants which require maintenance and ultimate replacement. Relatively inexpensive claddings can be used, avoiding complex prefabrication, or high on-site labour. Openings in open joint walling can, however, lead to quite complex detailing of catchment trays and shields (Figure 3/66).

EXPANSION JOINTS

Maintaining the weathertight integrity of a building shell demands that the wall surfaces should not be subjected to stresses which would cause cracking. It is, therefore, important that any movement likely to occur in a building shell should be quantified at design stage and allowance made in the shell for the movement to be taken up at specific joints designed to absorb it without fracture.

Movement can occur either within the walling element itself (its own thermal or moisture expansion and contraction), or between dissimilar materials of a structure (differential movement between cladding and struc-

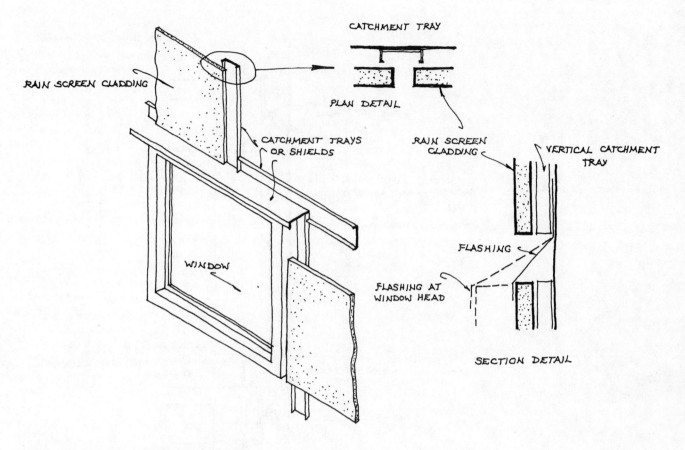

Figure 3/66 Opening in rain screen walling.

tural frame). These movements can also be either reversible (moisture and thermal), or non-reversible (shrinkage in concrete frames or components).

All walling materials suffer to some extent from thermal and/or moisture movements, but the monolithic walling (Type 1) suffers more obviously than that with light sheet claddings (Type 3). Sheet claddings tend to accommodate their thermal movement within the joints, which are designed accordingly. Some claddings such as plastic or aluminium siding, where the coefficients of expansion are high (6 to 7×10^{-5} per $^{\circ}$ C) require special precautions to be taken in the form of sliding fixings and larger end clearances. The manufacturer is the source of information on this subject and care should be taken to follow his advice.

In the case of Type 2 walling, the discontinuity of the panelized method of construction provides the building shell with sufficient joints to take up the amount of reversible movement normally encountered. A point of danger occurs where wall panels are trapped within the members of a concrete structure which will be subject to non-reversible shrinkage (Figure 3/67). This movement has to be accommodated by compressible filled joints at ledging positions and the fixings must be designed with expected movement in mind. It is unlikely that any movement will affect the integrity of the structural shell as such movement will normally be accommodated in the usual sealant filled or open joint.

Type 1 walling, on the other hand, can cause problems. Clay brickwork will, after an initial non-reversible expansion on absorbing moisture after kilning, suffer little reversible moisture movement. It has, however, a thermal expansion coefficient of between 4 and 8×10^{-6} per $^{\circ}$ C.

105

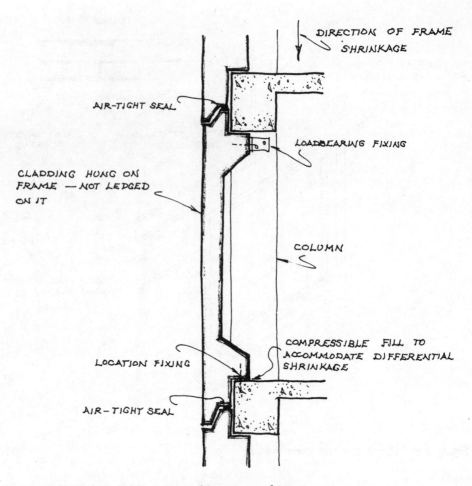

DIRECTION OF FRAME SHRINKAGE

AIR-TIGHT SEAL

LOADBEARING FIXING

CLADDING HUNG ON FRAME — NOT LEDGED ON IT

COLUMN

COMPRESSIBLE FILL TO ACCOMMODATE DIFFERENTIAL SHRINKAGE

LOCATION FIXING

AIR-TIGHT SEAL

Figure 3/67 Heavy claddings trapped in concrete frame.

Calcium silicate bricks have a reversible moisture movement of 0.05% and a thermal expansion coefficient of between 11 and 15 x 10^{-6} per ° C. This has led some authorities to make a distinction between clay and calcium silicate bricks with regard to the frequency of expansion joints. Straight walls of calcium silicate bricks should be broken approximately every 6 metres by expansion joints. Some authorities suggest that clay bricks should be similarly protected; others believe that for clay bricks this dimension can be doubled.

The movement in concrete blocks varies with the mix and type of aggregate used in their manufacture. Following an initial non-reversible shrinkage, which is common to all concrete elements, there is slight reversible moisture movement and a coefficient of thermal expansion of 7 to 10 x 16^{-6} per ° C. In order to overcome shrinkage and reversible movement problems, control joints are recommended in long straight walls at positions where cracking would be most likely to occur — abrupt changes in wall thickness or height, pipe chases, openings, junctions with columns, intersecting walls and any juxtaposition of dissimilar materials (Figure 3/68). Cracking is more likely to occur if the length of the panel exceeds about 1½ to 2 times its height. The shape of wall is more critical than the size. Blockwork walls should, as far as possible, be divided into rectangular panels without openings and with straight vertical control joints between panels.

Figure 3/69 illustrates various methods of detailing control joints in concrete blockwork. It should be noted that the sealant capping to the joint should be at least 12 mm deep and the sealant should be selected so that it has flexibility enough to accommodate the expected movement. Expansion joints in brickwork are usually somewhat simpler, being either a straight mortar joint scraped out to 12 mm depth on the exposed surfaces and filled with a polysulphide sealant, or a joint filler (compressible filler board of softwood fibres impregnated with bitumen, or cellular rubber filler sheet) which replaces the mortar behind the sealant (Figure 3/70).

The shrinkage of structural concrete frames when used with brick or block claddings should be accommodated by an expansion joint at the head

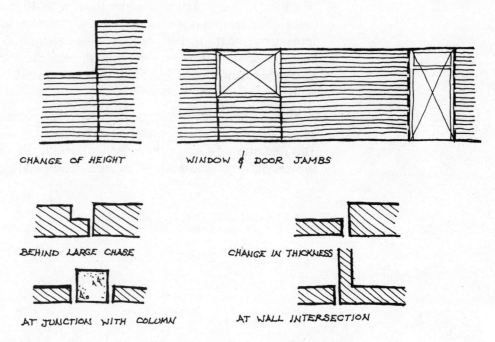

Figure 3/68 Positions of control joints in concrete block walls.

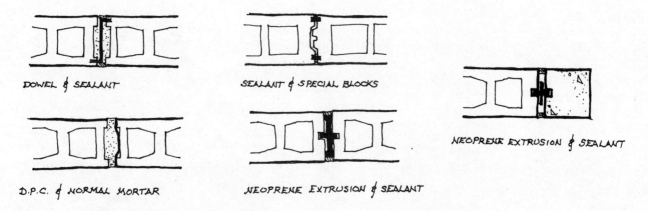

Figure 3/69 Methods of detailing control joints.

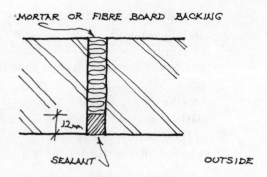

Figure 3/70 Expansion joint in brickwork.

of each storey-height lift of cladding (Figure 3/4). This necessitates the use of special restraint fixings in order to stabilize the head of the cladding panel while leaving it free in the vertical direction to be independent of frame movement. Similar points of high anticipated movement can occur below concrete flat roofs, where the thermal movement of the roof should be isolated from the wall in order to guard against possible cracking of the wall.

Building shells are not static monoliths but an assembly of parts, many of which are continuously moving at different rates and to different degrees. This fact must always be borne in mind and likely movement anticipated in the design, if the weathertight integrity of a building shell is to be preserved.

4 Roofs

The primary function of a roof, in all areas of the world except the most arid, is to provide a watertight cover to the building below. In so doing, it should not only present to the elements a surface that cannot be penetrated by water, but also shed as quickly as possible the water that falls on it.

As explained in Chapter 1, the logical and, from the point of view of water shedding, most functional shape of roof is one that is pitched – and pitched outwards, not inwards like that curious hybrid the butterfly roof. The pitched roof, however, is highly restrictive when one is planning large, complex buildings, so for these the flat roof becomes the only practical and economic form of roof.

Pitched roofs being the traditional roof shape in most countries, it is on the fundamental principles of the prevention of rain penetration rather than on the basic building construction details of these roofs that emphasis is placed here. In areas with rainy climates, however, flat roofs have a well-known reputation for leaking, so for these the construction details are more fully discussed.

The two forms of roof are dealt with in separate sections, as follows: –

1. Flat roofs: including those finished in asphalt, built-up bitumen felt and single membrane materials. Metal roofings (as well as metal faced felt) are discussed, although the cost of these coverings has well-nigh eliminated their use. A short section is included on glazed apertures.

2. Pitched roofs: including those covered in flat or contoured, large or small, interlocking or overlapping elements or in membrane finishes. Glazed areas are also included.

FLAT ROOFS

Flat roofs are a challenge. Though not the ideal roof shape for rainy climates they are sometimes necessary due to the complex plan forms of modern buildings. They are not easy to design – as evidenced by recent BRE statistics of flat roof failures – but if essential principles are followed they should be successful.

The expression 'flat roof' is misleading. In a rainy part of the world no roof should be laid flat, with the sole exception of the tanked asphalt roof, the design of which depends on the retention of water to provide protection for the roof covering. With this exception, therefore, the designer should always think of his roof not as a 'flat roof', but rather as a 'drained roof' — a roof consisting of a series of planes, the surfaces of which are designed to fall to drainage points — a series of very shallow double or mono-pitched roofs. In this way a roof will be produced that drains adequately and evenly to a series of points carefully spaced around or within the building area, and not to haphazardly spaced rainwater outlets which appear on the roof plan only at those points where fall pipes can be accommodated unobtrusively. When haphazard spacing is used, the inevitable result is a site foreman's nightmare of screeded falls, intersecting awkwardly, leading disproportionate amounts of water to some outlets and invariably leaving the odd area which is never drained at all. To provide a ratio of fall pipe area to roof area in accordance with the Building Regulations is not, in itself, sufficient; the fall pipes must be so spaced as to clear the whole roof surface of rainwater as quickly and evenly as possible.

The flat roof is a form involving more risk than a pitched roof, and this risk has to be eliminated by good design. Most of the failures of flat roofs are not inherent failures of the roof coverings, but are design failures. The starting point of good design is careful planning of the efficient removal of water from the roof area. Even minor defects in the roof covering can lead to disastrous results if the defects happen to be situated under a puddle! Standing water appreciably increases the risks, not only of leakage through a defective roof covering, but also by itself causing defects due to differential temperature build-up on the surface of the covering.

On simple buildings it is desirable for the drainage points to be outside the external face of the building. Under these conditions any minor defect in a fall pipe will not show up as a roof leak, causing internal damage to the building and aggravating the owner and occupants of the building. Internal rainwater pipes can cause problems out of all proportion to the size of the defect. If the problem were to occur outside the building shell, it would be quickly recognised, easily rectified and would cause no internal dislocation. External fall pipes may be architecturally less desirable than internal ones, but they are considerably less troublesome.

On complex buildings achievement of this ideal is obviously not possible. Where internal rainwater fall pipes are necessary they must be carefully designed to avoid blockages from fallen leaves, etc. (wire balloons should be fitted to the outlets); they should have few changes of direction, and any change should be gradual; they should be properly jointed and they should contain adequate cleaning plates through which any blockage can be removed.

Roof coverings

The primary object of a roof covering is to provide an impermeable layer which will protect the roof structure and the building below. Paradoxically, the impermeability of the roofing material is often a major contributory cause of flat roof failures. Because the outer covering is the most effective vapour barrier in many existing flat roof constructions, there is a very real danger of condensation forming on the under-side of this membrane (being on the 'cold-side' of the construction), leading to bubbling of the membrane and eventual failure. This problem will be dealt with more fully later in the chapter.

The principles involved in flat roof design and the causes of failure are common to all forms of roof covering. This being so, the coverings themselves will be discussed first, with illustrations typical of their effective use, then these will be related to the principles involved.

Roof coverings fall into two basic categories – jointless and jointed – each category including both hot and cold applications.

(a) Jointless coverings – hot

Asphalt

Asphalt used for roofing is usually limestone aggregate mastic asphalt to BS 988. It is applied in two layers to a total thickness on horizontal surfaces of 20 mm on an isolating layer of sheathing felt. Upstands (minimum 150 mm high) are formed of two layers with an overall thickness of 13 mm. BS Code of Practice CP 144: Part 4:1970, Roof Coverings; Mastic Asphalt, sets out recommendations for its use and methods of application. Asphalt is usually considered the best of all roofing membranes, but nevertheless is the most vulnerable to small movements in the underlying deck – hence

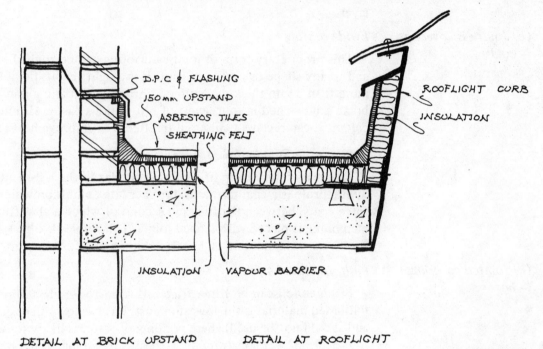

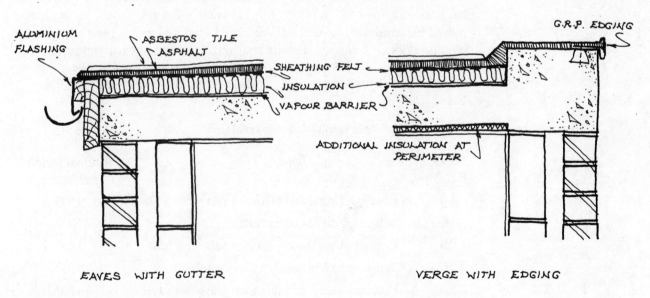

Figure 4/1 Typical asphalt roof details.

the need for a sheathing felt isolating layer. But however hard one tries to isolate the membrane, it is still anchored at the edges, at roof lights or where pipework passes through the roof. Complete isolation is impossible. It is recommended, therefore, that asphalt should never be used on the more 'lively' roof decks such as those of timber and metal.

In the past some roofs with asphalt covering were designed deliberately to retain a layer of water between 300 and 600 mm deep to protect the asphalt from solar radiation and high surface temperatures, to which it is vulnerable. It is very doubtful if this construction justifies the risk of leakage, the additional dead load and the consequent additional cost involved. Protection against solar radiation is, however, strongly recommended and should normally take the form of near-white asbestos tiles. Figure 4/1 illustrates a few typical details of asphalt roof coverings. Note the position of the vapour barrier in the examples — *underneath* the insulation layer.

(b) Jointless coverings — cold

Evode roofing

This proprietary form of jointless roofing can be applied to most decks and to any shape or profile of roof. It is a lightweight, flexible system not more than 3 mm thick made up of a priming coat and a reinforcing membrane sandwiched in four layers of bituminous paste. Although black in colour, it can receive a coloured treatment to improve heat reflectance.

Synthaprufe Standard Roofing System

This proprietary form of roofing is similar to the last-mentioned type. Synthaprufe is a coal tar/natural rubber latex emulsion which is applied in three coats, between the first and second of which a glass fibre reinforcing membrane is placed with lapped joints. The whole flexible system is finished with a blinding of 1.5 mm chippings before the top coat is set.

(c) Jointed coverings — hot

Built-up bitumen felt

Bitumen felt can be either fibre felt, asbestos or glass fibre based. Fibre felt based material is the lowest in cost, but has low dimensional stability and should not be used where ponding of water is likely to occur, or on roof decks of wet construction. Asbestos based material, on the other hand, has good dimensional stability and also greater fire resistance. Its use is required on combustible decks. Glass fibre based material is used in high quality work. It has good dimensional stability, will not rot and is non-absorbent. BS 747 designates bitumen felt in accordance with these base ingredients — fibre based, class 1; asbestos based, class 2; and glass fibre based, class 3.

Table 4/1   Roofing felts suitable for flat roofs

BS 747 Ref No	Type of felt	Nominal weight kg/10 m²
1B	Fine sand surfaced bitumen felt	17.0
1C	Self-finished bitumen felt	13.0
2B	Fine sand surfaced bitumen asbestos felt	16.0
2C	Self-finished bitumen asbestos felt	13.0
3B	Fine sand surfaced bitumen glass fibre felt	18.0
3G	Venting base layer bitumen glass fibre felt	32.0

Table 4/2 Roofing felt specifications for roof decks

Deck type	Reference	Description (BS 747 reference numbers)	External fire rating BS 476 Part 3
Concrete and screeded roofs, wood wool (prescreeded or prefelted), plywood	F1 fibre	(1) 2B or 2C PB (2) 1B or 1C FB (3) 1B or 1C FB Bitumen dressing 10 mm chippings	AA
	F2 asbestos	(1) 2B or 2C PB (2) 2B or 2C FB (3) 2B or 2C FB Bitumen dressing 10 mm chippings	AA
	F3 glass fibre	(1) 3B or 3G FB (2) 3B FB (3) 3B FB Bitumen dressing 10 mm chippings	AA
Dry insulation on decks, including metal	F4 fibre	(1) 1B or 1C FB (2) 1B or 1C FB (3) 1B or 1C FB Bitumen dressing 10 mm chippings	AA
	F5 asbestos	(1) 2B or 2C FB (2) 2B or 2C FB (3) 2B or 2C FB Bitumen dressing 10 mm chippings	AA
	F6 glass fibre	(1) 3B FB (2) 3B FB (3) 3B FB Bitumen dressing 10 mm chippings	AA
Timber boarding	F7 fibre	(1) 2B or 2C nailed (2) 1B or 1C FB (3) 1B or 1C FB Bitumen dressing 10 mm chippings	AA
	F8 asbestos	(1) 2B or 2C nailed (2) 2B or 2C FB (3) 2B or 2C FB Bitumen dressing 10 mm chippings	AA
	F9 glass fibre	(1) 2B or 2C nailed (2) 3B FB (3) 3B FB Bitumen dressing 10 mm chippings	AA

FB = fully bonded
PB = partially bonded

Three layers of felt bedded in hot bitumen are recommended for covering flat roofs. The upper surface of the felt is then finished with a bitumen dressing compound and at least 10 mm of stone chippings to provide protection from solar radiation. This thickness is substantially smaller than that obtaining in continental practice, where chippings are usually at least 50 mm thick. BS Code of Practice CP 144: Part 3:1970, Roof Coverings, Built-up Bitumen Felts, in addition to making recommendations on their usage and methods of application, sets down a schedule of available types and weights in table A2. Table 4/1 is a selection of those recommended for flat roof applications.

The Felt Roofing Conctractors Advisory Board sets out recommended specifications for various roof decks (Table 4/2) and if these specifications are followed a roof surface of long life expectancy will result under normal conditions. Abnormal conditions which could lead to breakdown will be discussed shortly.

Upstands and margins which are not protected by chippings should be protected by a coloured reflective coating. Figure 4/2 shows typical details of built-up felt roofing. Again, note the position of the vapour barrier.

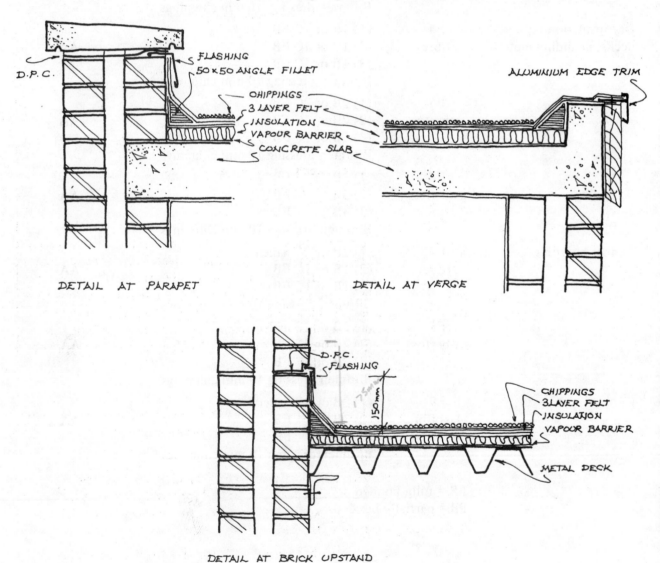

Figure 4/2 Typical built-up felt roof details.

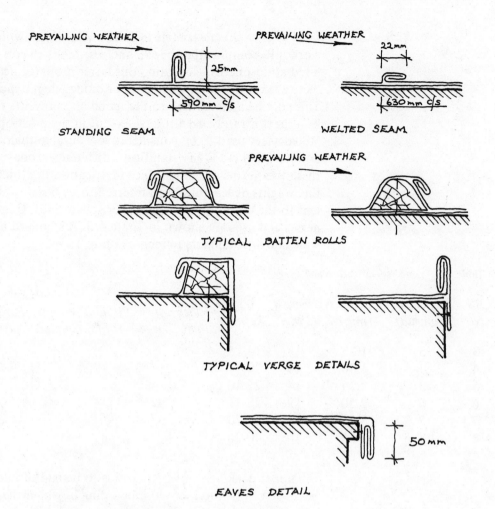

PREVAILING WEATHER

25mm

590mm c/s

STANDING SEAM

PREVAILING WEATHER

22mm

630mm c/s

WELTED SEAM

PREVAILING WEATHER

TYPICAL BATTEN ROLLS

TYPICAL VERGE DETAILS

50mm

EAVES DETAIL

Figure 4/3   Typical metal faced felt roof details.

Metal faced felt

This material combines the qualities of built-up roofing with the long-life characteristics of natural copper or aluminium sheet. When used as the top layer of a three layer specification, with the same falls as normal built-up roofing, it provides a roof of attractive appearance and achieves a fire designation of AA. It is fully bonded to the substructure, with all joints and seams fully sealed to eliminate wind drumming and work hardening. It should be laid in restricted lengths to allow for thermal movement without stress ageing. Figure 4/3 shows typical details.

Bitumen polymer

This is a single layer hot-laid roof covering, to which the comments later in this chapter concerning single layer sheet systems largely apply.

(d) Jointed coverings – cold

Fully supported sheet metal

Lead, copper, zinc and aluminium sheet can all be used as single layer roof finishes, or weathering surfaces. Being expensive, they are usually reserved for prestige work, or for those situations where a particular architectural effect is required.

Lead is a heavy metal, but because it is comparatively soft and has poor resistance to tearing or crushing, it must be used in relatively thick sheets. This factor must be considered in the design of the supporting decking.

Lead's other characteristics include malleability, which makes it easy to work into complicated shapes, and resistance to corrosion from most polluted atmospheres. Regarding this latter property, lead forms a tough protective surface film of carbonate or oxide when exposed to the atmosphere. This coating adheres well to the metal and prevents further corrosion. Cast lead sheet is rarely used today, except in the most opulent of buildings. Milled sheet used to be considered less durable than cast sheet, but it is doubtful if there is any significant difference, today, in the durability of these two forms of metal. Since metrication the thickness (and therefore the weight) of lead has been referred to by a series of BS numbers, equivalent to the old imperial weights per square foot. Comparable weights, thicknesses and uses are shown in Table 4/3. A standard metric sheet is 2.400 m wide and is obtainable in lengths up to 12 m.

Table 4/3 Lead: specification and usage

BS No	Wt per ft² (imperial)	Thickness (mm)	Nearest s.w.g.	Wt kg/m²	Uses						
					Flat roofs Small	Flat roofs Large	Pitched roofs	Valley gutters	Parapet gutters	Soakers	Dormers
3	3	1.25	18	14.18						√	
4	4	1.80	16	20.41	√					√	
5	5	2.24	14	25.40	√			√			
6	6	2.50	12	28.36	√	√	√	√	√		√
7	7	3.15	11	34.73		√	√		√		√
8	8	3.55	10	40.26							

Timber deckings on which lead is to be laid should fall 1:80 and should be made of plywood, or close boarding in which the boards are fixed in the direction of the fall or diagonally to it. Oak and elm boarding should be avoided as corrosion may result from chemical interaction with the lead. An underlay of butt jointed sarking felt or lapped building paper is always advisable to provide a separating layer between the lead and the decking, thereby ensuring ease of movement of the lead. Heavily impregnated bitumen felts are not suitable for underlays as in hot weather they soften and adhere to the lead, thus restricting its movement.

Careful detailing is required to minimise the effects of movement. The size of individual sheets should be restricted and their fixing should be such as to allow them to move without tearing. The latter requirement has led to the development of three types of joint for metal roofings — the roll, the drip and the welt — which, with minor variations, are suitable for all four metals. In the case of lead the problem of thermal movement is complicated by the characteristic of creep. As the temperature of the metal rises the sheet expands, but owing to its weight and its poor mechanical strength it does not contract by an equivalent amount when the temperature falls. Over the years, therefore, the sheet elongates and becomes thinner. This defect can be minimised by restricting sheet sizes.

On flat roofs no lead sheet should exceed 2.230 m² in area, or 3 m in length. Drips should be provided at sheet junctions across the fall, spaced on an average at 2.30 m centres (Figure 4/4). Preferably they should be 60 mm deep, but if provided with anti-capillary grooves they can be reduced to as little as 38 mm. Sheet junctions in line with the fall should be carried out by the use of timber batten rolls, spaced about 700 mm apart,

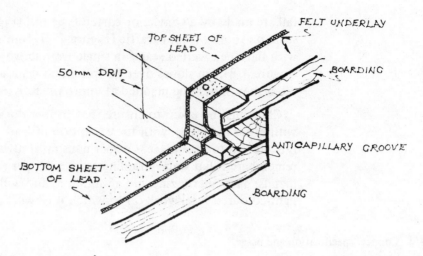

Figure 4/4 A lead drip.

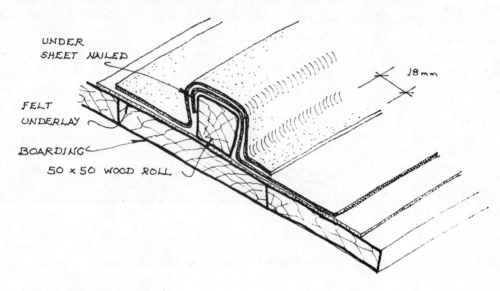

Figure 4/5 A lead roll.

50 mm x 50 mm in cross-section (Figure 4/5). On pitched roofs up to 50°, the division of the roof into bays should be similar to the division of flat roofs. Between 50° and 70° pitch the bay width should be limited to 533 mm and the length to 2.40 m. Bays of greater width would require extra fixings.

Copper, like lead is a heavy metal, but it has good mechanical strength together with good malleability. Because of its strength, it can be used in thin sheets; because of its malleability it can be formed into complicated shapes. Copper is resistant to attack by polluted atmospheres and on exposure it forms a thin coating of copper oxide on its surface, thereby preventing further attack. Copper has a useful life comparable to that of lead. Available thicknesses of sheet and strip copper and their uses are given in Table 4/4.

Sheet sizes available are 1.220 m x 610 mm and 1.830 m x 910 mm. Strip is supplied in any width up to 1.070 m, generally not cut to length.

Copper should be laid on deckings and underlays similar to those used for lead, and to a fall of not less than 1:60. Joints in the direction of the

117

fall are made by a conical or batten type roll (Figure 4/6), or a standing seam on roofs without traffic (Figure 4/7). Joints across the fall are formed with flattened welted seams, a single welt above 45°, a double welt below (Figure 4/8). On slopes over 10° pitch, no drips are necessary; below this pitch they should be planned at approximately 3 m intervals.

Care must be taken to ensure that copper does not come into contact with other metals as, with the exception of lead, they could cause electrolytic action to take place. Copper nails must always be used. It must be remembered that water draining from a copper roof will corrode other metals, particularly zinc and aluminium, and will also stain masonry and light-coloured brickwork on to which it flows.

Table 4/4 Copper: specification and usage

Thickness				Uses			
mm	s.w.g.	Roofing; pieces not exceeding 600 mm x 1.50 m	Roofing; pieces not exceeding 800 mm x 1.800 m	Gutters; max. 1.3 m² sheet	Gutters; max. 0.93 m² sheet	Soakers and secret gutters
0.6	23		✓	✓		
0.55	24		✓	✓		✓
0.45	26	✓			✓	

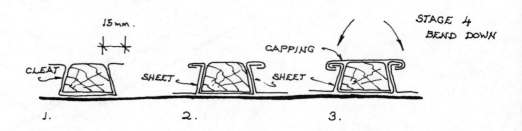

FOUR STAGES OF FORMING A BATTEN ROLL

FOUR STAGES OF FORMING A CONICAL ROLL

Figure 4/6 Conical and batten rolls (copper).

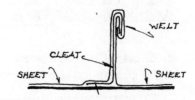

Figure 4/7 A standing seam.

118

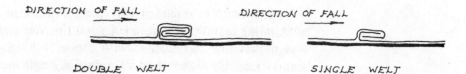

DOUBLE WELT   SINGLE WELT

Figure 4/8 Welts.

Zinc is not as malleable as lead or copper, but has good mechanical properties and is lighter than either of the other metals. Although zinc, too, forms a protective oxide coating on exposure, the film is not as dense or adherent as are those on copper or lead and, therefore, zinc does eventually corrode. As a roof covering it has a useful life of between 20 and 40 years, but zinc should never be used in heavily polluted areas.

Zinc sheet is traditionally supplied in zinc gauge sizes, those gauges produced in metric equivalents being given in Table 4/5.

Table 4/5 Zinc: specification and usage

Zinc gauge no.	Nearest s.w.g.	Thickness mm	Uses
12	23	0.6	Soakers
14	21	0.8	Roofing
16	19	1.0	Roofing

Metric sheet sizes are 1 m wide and multiples of 1 m in length.

Zinc can generally be laid on deckings and underlays similar to those used for the previously-mentioned metal roofings, but never on oak or western red cedar. Pitch or fall should be at least 1:64. Batten rolls and drips are used as for other metals and care should be taken to avoid electrolytic action between zinc and other metals. Nails and screws should either be of zinc, or be heavily galvanized.

Aluminium is one of the lightest metals. It has moderate mechanical strength and a malleability equal to that of copper. It is resistant to corrosion, forming a thin protective coating of aluminium oxide on exposure. As a fully supported roofing aluminium is used in thicknesses of 0.7 mm (22 g) and 0.9 mm (20 g) at a minimum fall of 1:60. The choice of gauge and grade depends on quality and type of work, as shown in Table 4/6.

Table 4/6 Aluminium: specification and usage

Material and grade to BS 1470	Thickness s.w.g.	Temper		Standing seam and roll
		Long strip system		
		Hand formed	Machine formed	
SI 99.99 grade	20	¼H	¼H	¼H
	22	½H	½H	½H
SIA 99.8 grade	20	0	¼H	0
	22	¼H	½H	¼H
SIB 99.5 grade	20	0	¼H	0
	22	¼H	½H	¼H
SIC 99 grade	20	0	¼H	0
	22	¼H	½H	0
NS 3 alloy	20	0	¼H	0
(1¼% manganese)	22	¼H	½H	0

Two alternative methods of fixing are used; the traditional *sheet system* of standing seams and batten rolls and the *long strip system*. The sheet system is similar to that used with copper — longitudinal joints as standing seams or batten rolls and lateral joints as single lock welts (on pitches over 40°) or double lock welts (between 5° and 40° pitch).

The long strip system uses strips up to 10.5 m long with standing seam longitudinal joints. Unlike the sheet system, in which the individual sheets are fixed at all edges, the strip system is fixed at the head of the slope and 3 m down the slope. Below this the standing seam is held by special sliding clips allowing freedom of thermal movement for the strip.

Table 4/7 gives a guide to the sizes of sheet or strip for different systems and gauges of metal.

Table 4/7 Aluminium: sheet sizes, systems and gauges

		Sheet system		Long strip system	
Thickness	Width	Length in m		Width	Length
		Flat roof	Pitched roof	mm	m
0.7 mm	457	3.660	2.440	457	10.670
(22 s.w.g.)	610	3.050	1.830		
0.9 mm	457	4.880	3.050	533	10.670
(20 s.w.g.)	610	4.270	2.440		

Single layer membranes

There are at present several single membrane roof coverings on the market. They are based on either an asbestos or a glass fibre backing and are finished with PVC or neoprene. The sheets are usually stuck down with adhesive to the deck and the junction between sheets is made by either gluing or cold welding a cover strip over the joint, cold welding being achieved by the use of a chemical solvent. Generally these materials are more expensive than built-up felt roofing, but their low site labour requirements, their resistance to ultra-violet light and their continued flexibility offer attraction. Some single layer coverings can be produced in light colours, which give good heat reflectivity. They can also be used on prefabricated units, which are merely taped together on site. Several of these materials have Agrément Certificates which suggest reliability, but their thickness (between 1.0 and 1.5 mm) and the dangers inherent in a single layer system, place enormous reliance on the material being perfect from manufacture, being undamaged during installation and the joints being entirely perfect. It would seem a reasonable precaution to increase the falls from those suggested for asphalt and built-up felt, in order to be assured of a quick despatch of water from the roof surface.

Prevention of failure in roof coverings

The root causes of most failures of roof coverings are common to all the types of roofing mentioned above. Failure rarely occurs solely due to faults in the waterproof membrane itself; it is usually due to poor detailing, or faulty design principles, which can result in

(a) movement in the deck below the roof membrane
(b) a build-up of water vapour below the membrane, or
(c) solar radiation damage to the membrane.

BRE Digest 8 states that built-up roofing could have a trouble-free life of about 20 years. Few such roofs do; but if splitting occurs within 10 years and the roofing specification was to the recommended standards, other causes than mere ageing need to be found.

An analysis of the causes of roof covering breakdown leads to the establishment of five basic principles which should be considered in the design of any flat roof.

1. The roof should drain

Ponding, caused by inadequate falls, will cause differential surface temperatures in the waterproof membrane, which will induce unacceptable stresses and eventually bring about the cracking of the covering. The Codes of Practice suggest a 'finished' fall of 1:80; but, allowing for building inaccuracy and structural deflection, it would be better for the designer to work to a planned fall of 1:40. This is in line with the Felt Roofing Contractors Advisory Board recommendations which are more stringent than those of the Code.

2. The roof covering must be protected from structural, thermal and moisture movement of the deck

All forms of roof are subject to movement − metal decks to thermal movement, timber decks to moisture movement, concrete decks to initial non-reversible shrinkage and continued reversible thermal movement. Such movement needs to be considered in relation to the choice of roof covering material. Asphalt, although the most expensive of coverings discussed, is least able to accommodate movement, even when laid on an isolating layer. It is not, therefore, recommended for use with timber or metal decks. BRE Digest 8 indicates that roofing felt tears at about 5% extension, therefore − allowing a safety factor − felt should not be used where it could be expected to have to withstand extension greater than 2%. Recommendations regarding movement and expansion joints are set down in BS Code of Practice CP 144.

Decks subject to thermal movement should be protected by placing the insulation above them, but the use of soft insulation immediately under the membrane should be avoided. Structurally, decks should be designed to avoid excessive movement when loaded, and abnormal deflection in any direction should be prevented. Timber boarded decks should be adequately nailed to avoid differential movement between boards. Normal joints in the continuity of the structure − construction joints, joints in decking or between precast units − should be recognised and treated as minor movement joints (Figure 4/9). Minor movement joints should occur at approximately 3 m intervals and should be capable of accommodating 3 mm of movement. Major expansion joints should be associated with expansion joints in the structure and should provide complete discontinuity (Figure 4/10).

3. Protection must be provided against solar radiation

Solar radiation causes deterioration in asphalt and built-up felt coverings. Reflective treatment is therefore required to minimise this deterioration by preventing excessive build-up of surface heat on the covering's naturally

Figure 4/9 **Minor movement joints.**

121

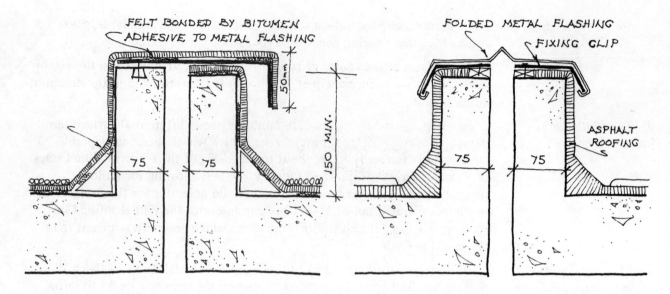

FELT DETAIL

ASPHALT DETAIL

Figure 4/10 Expansion joint.

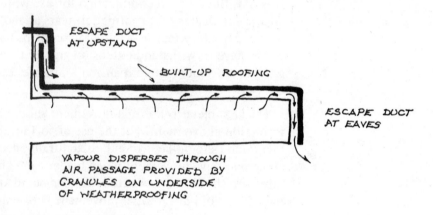

Figure 4/11 Ventilated underlay.

dark surfaces (a build-up encouraged by the fairly high levels of insulation of the underlying materials). Reflective treatments are particularly important in hot climates. White asbestos tiles make a good reflective layer for asphalt; white stone chippings for built-up felt. If the roof is accessible, concrete tiles may be justified — certainly in areas of anticipated point loading, such as may be produced by window cleaner's ladders. Upstands should also be treated. Brush-applied reflective coatings may be used, but these are, unfortunately, expensive to maintain. An alternative treatment for these areas, initially more expensive but with considerably less maintenance cost, is the use of metal faced felt.

4. Entrapped construction water must be allowed to escape

Construction water can come from the concrete deck, from the screed or from damp insulation. Once the membrane is installed the construction water cannot escape and it is drawn to the underside of the membrane where it vapourises, causing blistering of the membrane. If the screed is below the vapour barrier and final insulation, it is possible to drain the construction water downwards through pipes cast into the concrete slab. Where screeds are above the vapour barrier, it is advisable that they are not mixed

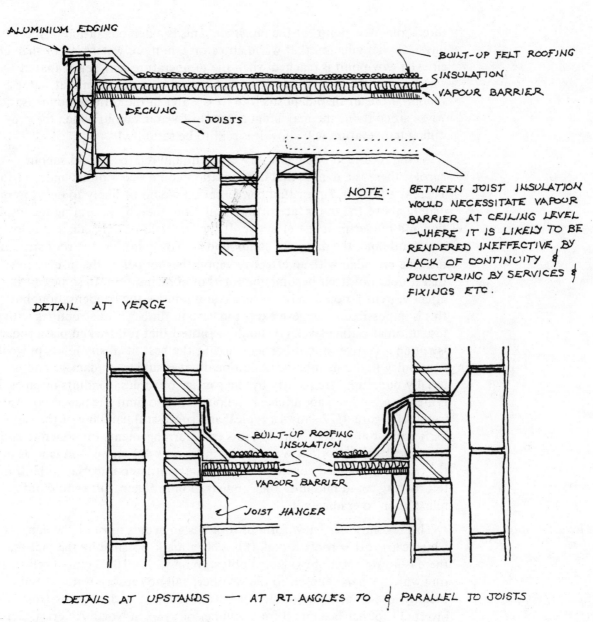

ALUMINIUM EDGING

BUILT-UP FELT ROOFING

INSULATION

VAPOUR BARRIER

DECKING   JOISTS

NOTE: BETWEEN JOIST INSULATION WOULD NECESSITATE VAPOUR BARRIER AT CEILING LEVEL —WHERE IT IS LIKELY TO BE RENDERED INEFFECTIVE BY LACK OF CONTINUITY & PUNCTURING BY SERVICES & FIXINGS ETC.

DETAIL AT VERGE

BUILT-UP ROOFING

INSULATION

VAPOUR BARRIER

JOIST HANGER

DETAILS AT UPSTANDS — AT RT. ANGLES TO & PARALLEL TO JOISTS

Figure 4/12   Vapour barrier in timber roof.

with water. Lightweight water-mixed insulating screeds laid over the vapour barrier should be avoided at all costs, because this form of construction results in construction water trapped between vapour barrier and roofing membrane. Precisely the same situation is produced if board insulation in this position is allowed to get wet during construction. Bitumen based lightweight aggregate insulating screeds can be laid over a felt and hot bitumen vapour barrier, but should be protected from rain until the roof covering is laid. A ventilated underlay in a built-up felt covering will help to relieve trapped construction water (Figure 4/11), but should not be relied upon as the sole solution to the problem. The problem should be solved by careful and informed designing.

5. Condensation must be prevented from forming below the roofing membrane

Condensation below the roofing membrane has the same effect as entrapped construction water. Humidity is generally higher inside an occupied building than outside. Water vapour will therefore pass through the structure of a building and condense out at that point where the tempera-

123

ture is the 'dew-point' of the moist air. This is a demonstration of the physical phenomenon that warm air can retain more water vapour than cold air. The dew-point is reached when the temperature falls below that at which air with a given quantity of water vapour can contain that water vapour — the air then deposits its excess water in the form of condensation. When air contains the maximum amount of water vapour which the prevailing temperature will allow it is said to be saturated.

As the roof membrane is a very efficient and relatively cold vapour barrier, there is a danger that condensation could occur on its under surface. There is a further danger that condensation would be likely to occur immediately above the outer face of the insulation, thereby saturating the insulation and rendering it less effective. If the insulation is immediately below the membrane, the danger is compounded. To avoid this, the roof structure must be provided with an effective vapour barrier *below* the insulation so that it does not itself become the focus of condensation. In some cases, effective ventilation of a roof space could remove the condensation; but this is impossible to achieve except in certain timber roof structures with insulation at ceiling level. (It should be noted that foil-backed plasterboard is *not* an effective vapour barrier since, at the best, its many joints prevent continuity in the membrane. Additionally it is subject to damage and is usually punctured frequently by the passage of cables, conduits or pipes. It is merely a modest vapour check, helping only to limit the passage of water vapour.) Figure 4/12 shows a typical and successful handling of the vapour barrier in a timber roof. Similar, successful arrangements for concrete and metal deck constructions were shown in Figures 4/1 and 4/2. Again, as in the case of entrapped construction water, a ventilated underlay in built-up felt roofing could minimise the condensation problem, but should not be relied upon to eradicate it.

The inverted roof

This revolutionary new form of roof design avoids most of the dangers which cause other roofs to fail. It has been made possible by the fact that there is now a form of expanded polystyrene with a 100% closed cell structure which, when exposed to the weather, will not absorb water — and thereby lose its insulating value, or become subject to damage by frost. The inverted roof has been used for a number of years in North America, Germany and Switzerland and it is from this experience over at least 7 years that claims for the material are made. It has been discovered from tests on actual buildings that water absorption in the polystyrene has been less than 0.1% by volume. This has led the GLC and the DOE to accept this method of roof construction, subject to the correct type of expanded polystyrene being used.

The basis of the roof is the removal of the insulation to a position above the roofing membrane. In other words, the membrane (asphalt or built-up felt) is laid directly on the screeded roof slab. It is then covered with loose-laid expanded polystyrene slabs with broken joints. The polystyrene is held in position and protected by a 50 mm layer of gravel or (in the case of access ways) by paving slabs on felt corner pads (Figure 4/13). Because the membrane is laid on the dimensionally stable deck, rather than the less stable insulation, damage is less likely. It is fully protected from solar radiation. Entrapped construction water will dry out downwards after the insulation is installed. The roofing membrane forms the vapour barrier itself — no separate vapour barrier is required — but because it is on the 'warm side'

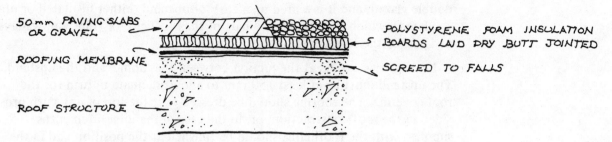

Figure 4/13 Inverted roof – cross section.

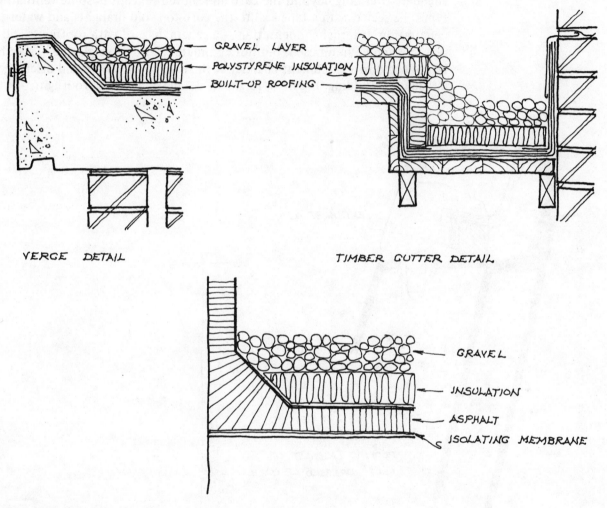

VERGE DETAIL

TIMBER GUTTER DETAIL

Figure 4/14 Typical details of inverted roof.

of the insulation, no condensation will take place. The method also has advantages with regard to site organisation, being a process less at the mercy of the weather than others, and has few maintenance requirements. Some typical details are shown in Figure 4/14. It seems likely that this form of construction could lead to a much greater life expectancy for roof coverings.

Glazed apertures

Glazed apertures in flat roofs are today usually constructed with rooflights rather than with the now old-fashioned and expensive lantern light built up in patent glazing. Common forms are a square or a rectangular single unit with a 'dome' (flat, pyramidal or curved) fabricated in acrylic, GRP, PVC or glass. This 'dome' can be either wired or unwired, single or

125

double glazed, and it is seated on a curb or upstand (either insulated or un-insulated), which is designed as a part of the rooflight, or (rarely nowadays) as a part of the roof construction.

Leakage risk occurs at the juction between the 'dome' and the upstand. The upstand must be at least 150 mm to allow adequate upturn for the roof covering. The roofing should be dressed over the top of any curb provided in the roof construction, or, in the case of manufactured curbs supplied with the rooflights, should be finished at the position and in the manner recommended by the manufacturer. The 'dome' should have an adequate overhang beyond the curb and should (except in some ventilating types) be sealed with a tape seal to the curb to avoid draughts and water penetration. Internal condensation – a general hazard with rooflights and one that can be minimised, but not eliminated, by double glazing – should be collected in a catchment channel at the base of the dome and discharged outside the building. Figure 4/15 shows details of a typical rooflight.

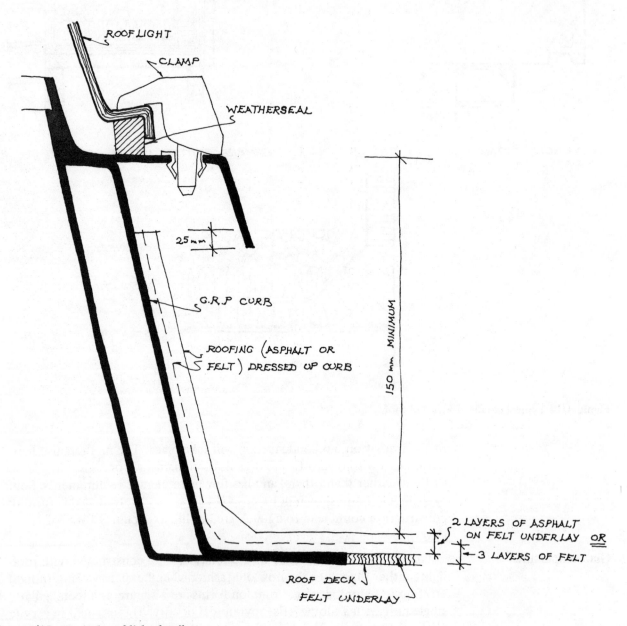

Figure 4/15 Typical roof light details.

Rooflight design has, in the past, received too little attention — hence the dissatisfaction, with regard to leakage, with some products on the market. There is in the UK neither a recognised test method to ascertain a rooflight's performance nor a method of grading products against performance standards. The only performance requirements currently documented are those of thermal insulation. As a result, the design with regard to air and water leakage of many types of rooflight (especially when these are used in exposed positions) often leaves much to be desired. Any opening at high level in a building is vulnerable to air and rain penetration. As has been explained earlier, even small increases in height markedly affect exposure conditions. Rooflights, then, are particularly vulnerable and warrant a more satisfactory method of design than the empirical method that has been employed up to now.

PITCHED ROOFS

The roof coverings of pitched roofs may be classified under two broad catergories:—

(a) jointed roofings laid in hot bitumen, similar to those already discussed in the previous section;

(b) roofings made up of units whose junctions are unsealed and which rely on multiple thicknesses, broken joints or interlocking profiles to provide weathertightness.

The minimum acceptable slope of a pitched roof is dictated by its type of covering, and for category (b) roofs it is particularly critical. Some of the smaller unit coverings in this category (tiles and slates) are not necessarily in themselves watertight under all conditions and rely on a layer of sarking felt to give a final defence. Larger interlocking units (asbestos and metal sheets) do not require this secondary safeguard, but their satisfactory performance is dependent on the correct minimum pitch being used. Joints are generally unprotected by seals, and depend on the geometry of the side lap and the slope of the roof to preserve the integrity of the covering.

Details of pitched roof coverings can be found in almost any book on building construction, and recent developments in this particular area of building technology have not been dramatic. This being the case, in this book it is on the principles involved rather than on precise details of construction that attention will be focussed.

Roof coverings

(a) Jointed coverings laid in hot bitumen

Built-up felt

Jointed coverings on pitched roofs are usually restricted to built-up felt, with a top layer of either mineral finished or metal faced felt. Most of the comments on built-up felt used for flat roofs apply equally to pitched roof applications, except where they concern the top layer. For pitched roofs, to the list of recommended felts in the flat roof section should be added the list of top layers given in Table 4/8.

In terms of built-up roofing, a pitched roof is one of 5° pitch or over. Below that pitch the specifications in the previous section apply. Between 5° and 10° pitch the final finish can be either a bitumen dressing and stone chippings (as for a flat roof), or a mineral surfaced felt. Over 10° the mineral surfaced felt (or metal faced felt) should always be used.

Recommended roofing specifications for pitched roofs, by the Felt Roofing Contractors Advisory Board, are given in Table 4/9, from which it will be noted that either two or three layer specifications are suitable for sloping roofs. The three layer specification is, however, preferable.

It is essential that the roof space of timber and wood wool decked pitched roofs should be ventilated to avoid the build-up of condensation.

Table 4/8   Top layers for built-up felt on pitched roofs

BS 747 Ref No	Type of felt	Nominal weight kg/10 m²
1E	fibre based mineral surfaced bitumen felt	36.0
2E	asbestos based mineral surfaced bitumen felt	36.0
3E	glass fibre based mineral surfaced bitumen felt	27.0

Table 4/9.   Roofing felt specifications for pitched roofs.

Deck Type	Reference	Description (BS 747 reference numbers)		External fire rating BS 476 Part 3
Concrete and screeded roofs, wood wool (prescreeded or prefelted), plywood	S1 fibre	(1) 2B or 2C (2) if required 1B or 1C (3) 1E	PB FB FB	AC (concrete or wood wool) CC (plywood)
	S2 asbestos	(1) 2B or 2C (2) if required 2B or 2C (3) 2E	PB FB FB	AB
	S3 glass fibre	(1) 3B or 3G (2) if required 3B (3) 3E	PB FB FB	AB
Dry insulation on decks, including metal	S4 fibre	(1) 1B or 1C (2) if required 1B or 1C (3) 1E	FB FB FB	AC
	S5 asbestos	(1) 2B or 2C (2) if required 2B or 2C (3) 2E	FB FB	AB
	S6 glass fibre	(1) 3B (2) if required 3B (3) 3E	FB FB FB	AB
Timber boarding	S7 fibre	(1) 2B or 2C (2) if required 1B or 1C (3) 1E	nailed FB FB	CC
	S8 asbestos	(1) 2B or 2C (2) if required 2B or 2C (3) 2E	nailed FB FB	AB
	S9 glass fibre	(1) 2B or 2C (2) if required 3B (3) 3E	nailed FB FB	AB

FB = fully bonded. PB = partially bonded.

Small, non-interlocking units (flat tiles and slates)

It is generally true that the smaller the roofing unit, the steeper the minimum pitch and the more intricate the lapping required to obtain a weathertight covering. All coverings in this category rely in more exposed conditions on a layer of sarking felt to act as a final check to water ingress. A relatively recent development of sarking felt is insulating felt which significantly improves the insulation of the roof space and reduces the likelihood of condensation. This felt consists of a 50 mm mat of rockwool fibres sandwiched between a rot-resistant vapour barrier on the underside and a sheet of flexible polyethylene on the outer face. It is manufactured with a lapping selvedge on both edges (vapour barrier one side, polyethylene the other), so that at each horizontal joint the insulation is butted and outer sheets are lapped (Figure 4/16). It is fixed in the conventional manner, nailed with clout nails to the rafters, allowing a 75 mm sag between to allow seepage to drain down the roof and away at the eaves, where the polyethylene selvedge is nailed over the tilting fillet and the top of the fascia board.

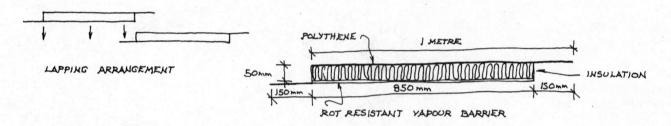

Figure 4/16 Insulated sarking felt.

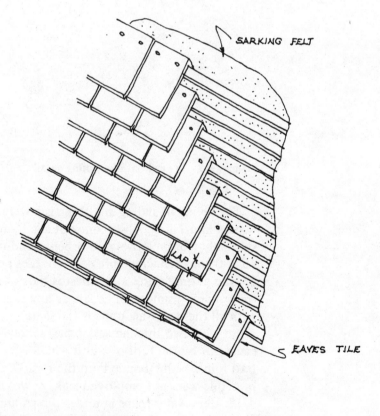

Figure 4/17   Flat tile roofing.

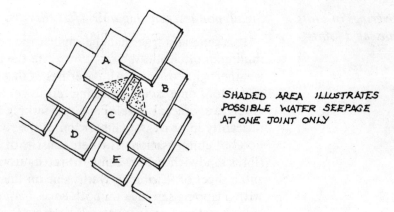

SHADED AREA ILLUSTRATES
POSSIBLE WATER SEEPAGE
AT ONE JOINT ONLY

Figure 4/18   Insufficient lap of tiles.

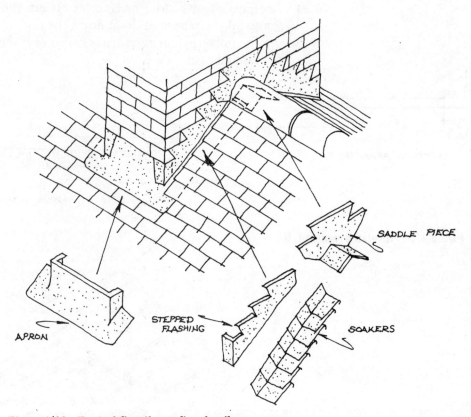

SADDLE PIECE

APRON

STEPPED
FLASHING

SOAKERS

Figure 4/19   Typical flat tile roofing details.

The laying of slating and tiling is covered by BS Code of Practice 142: Slating and Tiling. Absorbency of small, non-interlocking units varies substantially from relatively absorbent hand-made clay tiles (minimum pitch 45°), through machine pressed clay tiles and concrete tiles (minimum pitch 35°) to natural slates and asbestos slates which are highly impermeable (large natural slates can be laid as low as 25° pitch). The principle applied with all these roofing units is the same — at every point in the roof there are at least two thicknesses of tile, achieved by an overlap of the head of each unit by the foot of a unit which is two courses higher, and by side butt joints being 'bonded' up the roof slope (Figure 4/17). If the double lap principle were not employed leakage would occur, as illustrated in Figure 4/18. Here water seeps in under tiles A and B and over tile C and runs in above the head of tiles D and E.

In the case of flat tiles (BS 402 Part 2:1970 (Clay) and BS 473 & 550 Part 2: 1971 (Concrete)), there is a range of matching hip, valley and ridge tiles available and flashings to upstands are undertaken using metal or other proprietary flashings and soakers. Some typical details are illustrated in Figure 4/19.

Natural slating (BS 680:Part 2:1971) is becoming rare nowadays, due to its initial cost and the weight it imposes on the roof structure. Slate is, however, almost completely non-absorbent and has a long life expectancy. Head nailing is usually employed, except in exposed areas on pitches below 30° or with long slates. In these cases there would be a danger of the wind tending to strip the slates off the roof, therefore centre nailing is employed to avoid this. The disadvantage of centre nailing is that there is only one layer of slate above the nail position, rather than two in the case of head nailing (Figure 4/20).

Fully compressed asbestos slates (to BS 690:Part 1:1963) have tended to replace natural slates in most applications. They are cheaper, and by being lighter they also cheapen the roof structure.

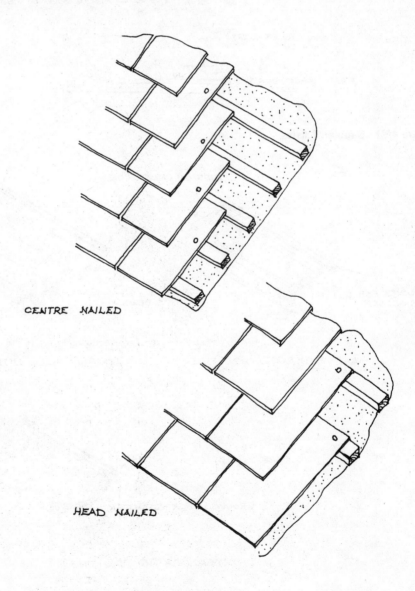

CENTRE NAILED

HEAD NAILED

Figure 4/20 Head nailed and centre nailed slating.

131

A form of simulated slate which is, in fact, a series of bitumen felt strips (BS 747:Type 1E) is also available. These are produced in 1m lengths in a beaver tail or square butt pattern (Figure 4/21) and are nailed to 19 mm T & G boarded roofs. In exposed situations the tails of the slates are stuck down with mastic. They provide a light, watertight covering on a pitched roof of not less than 30° slope; but their fire designation is only CC, unless they are backed by two nailed layers of asbestos based felt, when it is improved to BC.

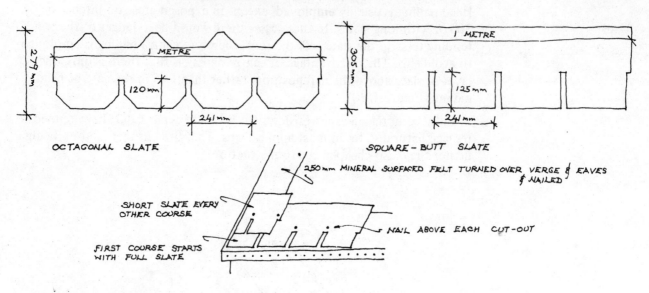

Figure 4/21 Simulated slates.

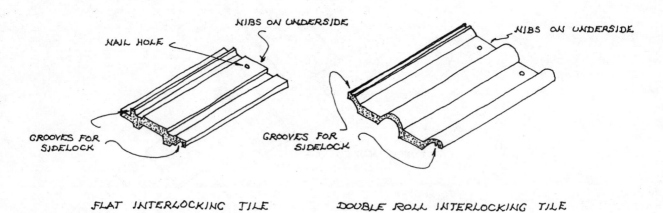

Figure 4/22 Interlocking tiles.

Small interlocking units (pan tiles, interlocking, single and double lap tiles).

There is a wide variety of interlocking tiles on the market. Some more recently developed can achieve watertightness at quite shallow pitches. These tiles are used in conjunction with sarking felt. The first English form of this type of tile was the pan tile. It is a single lap tile, whose edge profile provides an interlock with the side of the adjoining tile (Figure 4/22). From this have been developed many proprietary forms of interlocking clay and concrete tile. The manufacturer's recommendations should be followed regarding their use.

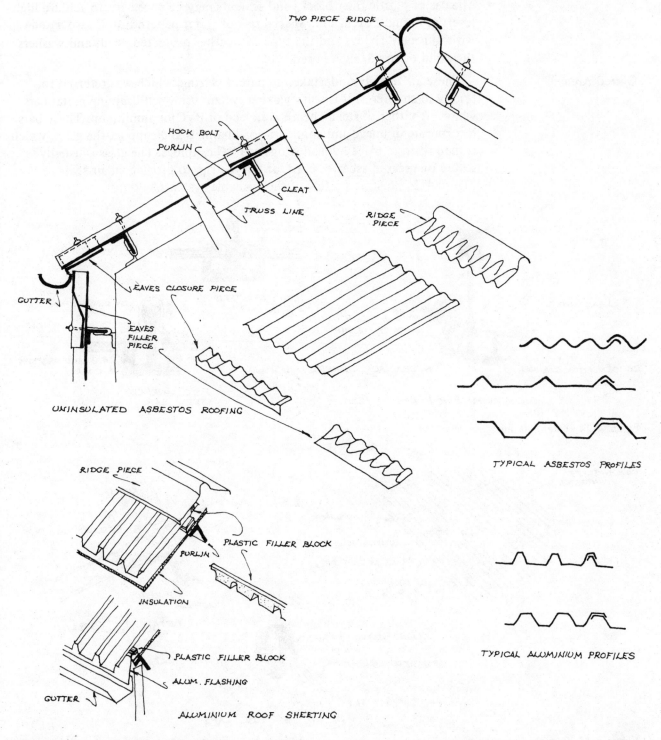

Figure 4/23 Corrugated sheet roofing — typical details.

Large interlocking units (corrugated asbestos and metal sheets)

Vast numbers of profiled asbestos (BS 690:Part 1:1963 and Part 3:1973) and metal (BS 3083:1959 and BS 4868:1972) cladding and roofing sheets are currently available. They are completely impervious and achieve their weathertightness by a horizontal overlap and by interlocking profiles on their vertical junctions. No sarking felt is required with these materials, but the manufacturer's recommendations regarding minimum pitch must be followed. Pitches as low as 12½° are possible. There are matching profiled fillers, corner and ridge pieces, barge boards and flashings (Figure 4/23). The use of plastic filler blocks and sealants may be necessary to achieve high levels of draught exclusion. Special risk of water penetration is associated with 'through' fixings and the type of weather protected heads and washers shown in Figure 3/59 are used.

Glazed Areas

These are usually undertaken in patent glazing, which was referred to briefly in chapter 3. It is a dry glazing system using self-draining metal bars which are either of steel (sheathed in lead or PVC)or aluminium. These bars incorporate drainage and condensation channels and support the glass, which is then fixed in place by lead wings or PVC cappings. The glass is usually seated on greased asbestos cord, or butyl strip, to provide an air seal. Figure 4/24 illustrates a few of the available systems.

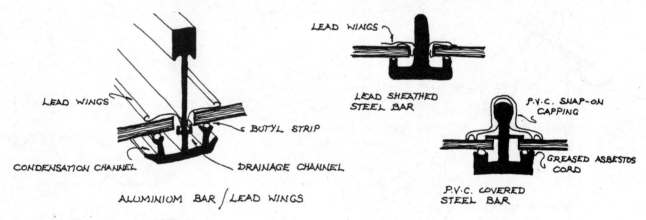

Figure 4/24 Patent glazing systems.

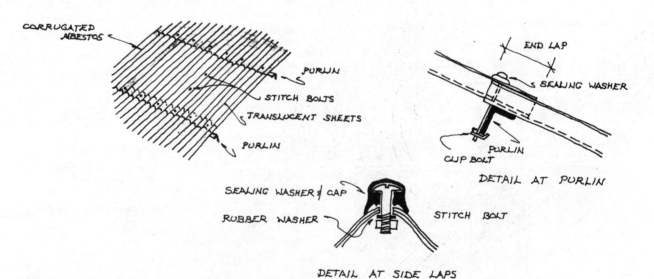

Figure 4/25 Translucent sheeting details.

Patent glazing is covered by BS Code of Practice 145. It will usually remain weathertight down to a 15° pitch, the glazing bar forming a two-stage joint — the wings act as water deflectors and the drainage channel disposes of whatever leakage occurs. Glazing can be either single or double and opening sections can be included.

Glazing can be incorporated in corrugated roofs by means of translucent sheets (polyester, glass fibre and PVC) of matching corrugations. Mastic or foam strips are often used to protect the side laps from water infiltration (Figure 4/25).

5 Remedial Treatments and Weatherstripping

This chapter deals with straightforward remedial treatments which can be undertaken without major disruption to the working of a building. Many failures in the weathertightness of structural shells, however, are difficult to trace (there is a leak, but precisely what is leaking?) and in their rectification involve considerable replacement or reconstruction of the building shell. For instance, a leaking or permeable wall can be treated by building an additional skin on the exterior with a cavity between the new work and the old; by rendering the wall with sand and cement or providing a similar impervious skin; or by rebuilding the wall, even; whilst the splitting of a built-up felt roof could be caused by a wrongly positioned vapour barrier, to correct which could be either a small or a large task depending on the construction of the roof. It could involve a total re-roofing of the building. Remedial treatments of this scale are beyond the scope of this chapter; as, also, are treatments which would be deduced from the recommendations made in the foregoing chapters, e.g. replacement of a faulty sealant by one more appropriate to the conditions of a particular joint.

Remedial treatments discussed here will deal with problems which are not of a nature requiring any major re-construction, although they could be very annoying and may even render a building unsuitable for use. They are remedies which can be carried out relatively simply. For instance the waterproofing of an old slate roof which has become porous can, in some circumstances, be undertaken without re-slating the roof — thus avoiding a major operation that would inconvenience the occupants of the building. It is the simpler and less inconvenient of the two alternatives which is discussed here. It need not be the better of the alternatives so long as it is a valid remedial treatment.

Remedial work may be placed in two categories: one concerning the primary elements of a building (the walls and roof) and the other concerning the secondary elements (doors and windows). The first includes such work as the rendering of a leaking wall or roof, or part of a wall or roof, to make it watertight without resort to rebuilding. The second consists largely of weatherstripping or draughtproofing work.

PRIMARY ELEMENTS: WALLS

Failure in the weathertightness of a wall can be caused by water penetrating through the walling material itself, due either to initial porosity

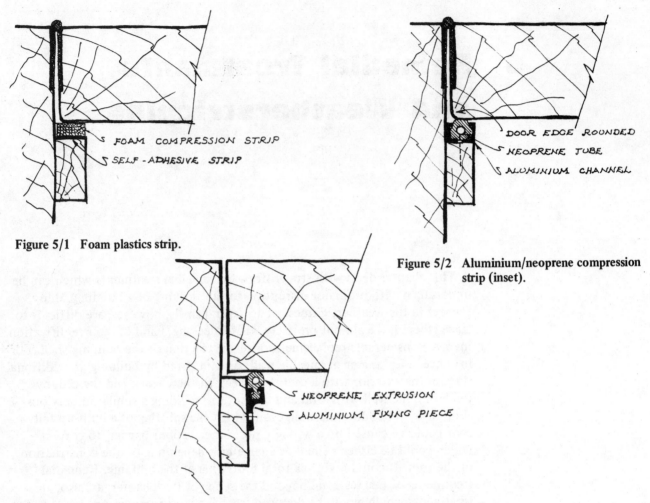

Figure 5/1   Foam plastics strip.

Figure 5/2   Aluminium/neoprene compression strip (inset).

Figure 5/3   Aluminium/neoprene compression strip (planted-on).

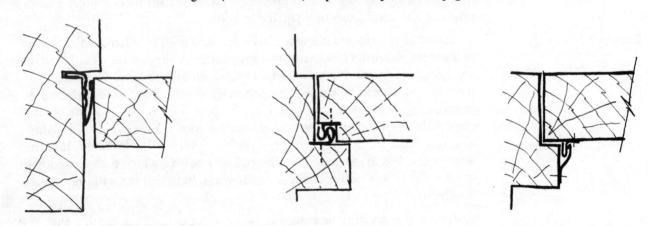

Figure 5/4   Metal spring strip devices.

or to porosity caused by deterioration through age. It can also be caused by joint failure of various types — deteriorating mortar joints, failure of sealant joints between walling units or failure in sealant or mortar joints between the walling and secondary elements. Such joint failures can be remedied relatively easily, assuming that the original design does not place unreasonable strains on the jointing medium — strains that could not be borne even by a substitute, more resilient medium. For the simplest form of joint failure (mortar deterioration) mere re-pointing will probably solve the problem.

138

Care should be taken, however, to ensure that the correct cause of leakage is established. The true cause of a failure may not be readily appreciated and the most obvious conclusion is not necessarily the right one. For instance, take the case of dampness on the inside of a window reveal. The obvious cause would be a breakdown in the mortar joint between the frame and the brick cavity wall, for which the remedy might be the replacement of the mortar joint by a non-setting sealant. However, breakdown of that joint may not be the problem. Failure could, in fact, be caused by moisture by-passing the damp proof membrane at the reveal where the cavity is closed, which, in turn, could be due to a faulty damp-proof membrane or to the wrong placing of the window in relation to the damp-proof membrane. Tracing the real cause of a fault is not always easy. Each case must be considered with great care in order to avoid expenditure on abortive remedies. For instance, in some cases of apparent water penetration dampness may actually be caused by internal condensation.

Simple remedial treatments for walls fall into two main groups – the replacement of sealants to joints and the treatment of porous walls. Treatments in the first group are self-explanatory, although not always easy to carry out – for example, the replacement of a neoprene gasket between precast concrete wall panels, unless planned for at the design stage, can be a difficult task. The treatment of porous walls requires the use of one of a range of proprietary products developed particularly for the purpose. These are of two types:—

a) transparent films for external application

b) non-transparent membranes for internal application (or external application where appearance is not important).

Transparent film products have been developed specifically for the purpose; some of the non-transparent membranes have been developed from cold damp-proof jointless membranes used in sandwich floor construction and wall tanking below ground level.

Transparent coatings

Transparent coatings have been developed for application on the exterior of porous walls to seal their surfaces and repel rainwater without markedly altering the appearance of the walls. They are either brush or spray applied to clean and sound surfaces of brick, masonry or concrete, and are based on either silicone resins (as covered in BS 3826:1969) or epoxy resins. Some silicone based products are not recommended for application to limestone.

Silicone-based products are usually effective when applied in one liberal coating on all but the most porous surfaces. Two coats will be required on very porous surfaces. They should **not** be applied to mastics or over painted surfaces (except cement paint). Often they are treated with a fugitive dye which, while allowing treated surfaces to be identified immediately after application, will disappear within a week.

Epoxy resin coatings are two part applications – Part A being a pigmented aqueous dispersion of a polyamide curing agent, Part B a dispersion of epoxy resin. The two parts are measured in the correct proportions and mixed together thoroughly. The resultant coating is then brushed generously on to the wall, usually in two applications. When mixed, the coating has a pot life from ½ hour at 38°C to 3 hours at 15°C. It dries to form a tough, clear coating with (unlike the silicone-based products) an ability to withstand a hydrostatic pressure in excess of 275 kN/m² (28 m head of water). This

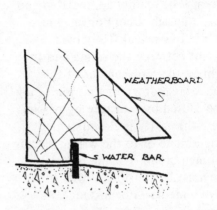

Figure 5/5 Traditional weatherboard and water bar.

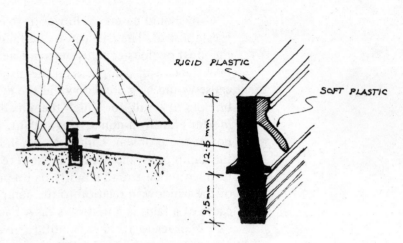

Figure 5/6 Compression water bar.

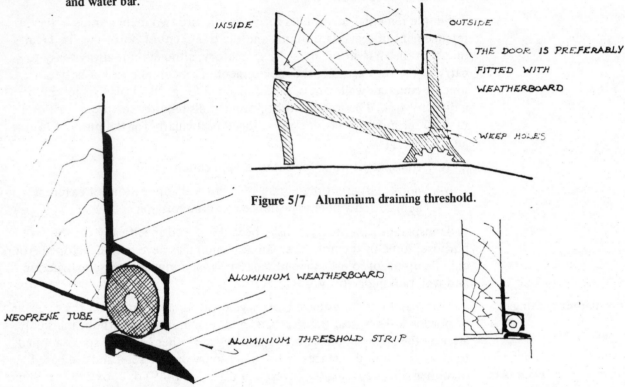

Figure 5/7 Aluminium draining threshold.

Figure 5/8 Aluminium/neoprene compression weatherboard.

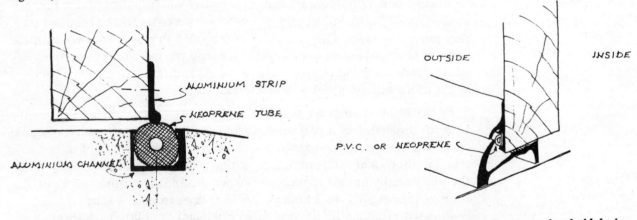

Figure 5/9 Aluminium/neoprene compression threshold device.

Figure 5/10 Two-part threshold device.

characteristic makes the product useful for internal application where ground water pressure is anticipated through the wall.

It should be remembered that these treatments do not have any marked bridging capacity, and any cracks in the walling should be cut out and pointed in cement mortar before the coating is applied. As specific products have their own particular characteristics, the manufacturer's instructions should be followed at all times.

Non-transparent membranes

Non-transparent membranes differ from transparent coatings in that they form a membrane of a more substantial thickness (usually between 1 mm and 2.5 mm) on the treated wall and have a significant bridging capacity (some being able to bridge cracks up to 1.5 mm wide). Many have been developed from the multi-coat, jointless, cold-applied membranes used in sandwich solid floor construction or in tanking below ground level. Some can be used without protection on surfaces subjected to traffic, others would need protection; some are black in appearance, others may be a decorative colour.

They are usually based on tar/rubber, tar extended polyurethane, polyurethane resin or epoxy resin. Most can be applied internally or externally. When a membrane is applied internally, old plaster which is badly rotted through dampness has to be removed, the wall is then skimmed over with cement mortar to produce a smooth surface and the membrane applied in the recommended number of coatings. In some cases the final coat can be blinded with clean, sharp sand to provide a key for new plaster. The epoxy resin based membranes are two part applications which are treated as explained in the section on transparent coatings. They have a pot life of from 1 hour at 40°C to 3½ hours at 15°C. When cured, this type of membrane froms a tough coating with a hydrostatic pressure resistance in excess of 275 kN/m².

The products in this category vary substantially and the manufacturer's recommendations should be followed in every case.

PRIMARY ELEMENTS: ROOFS

Leaking roofs (flat or pitched) are usually the result of deterioration of the roof covering (cracking of old built-up roofing felt,)deterioration of slates causing porosity, etc.), or the deterioration of internal gutters (cracking of old lead lining to parapet gutters, etc.). A cure can be effected either by stripping off the old roofing and then re-roofing, with consequent high costs and inconvenience, or by a remedial treatment involving the use of one of the cold-applied, jointless membranes referred to in chapter 4. These multi-layer treatments can be applied direct to existing roof finishes of bitumen felt, asphalt, lead, slate or corrugated roofing — provided that the following points are observed.

The roof covering must be complete — missing and loose slates or sheets must be replaced or re-fixed. Surfaces must be cleaned thoroughly. Cracks to flat roofs must be thoroughly raked out and given extra coatings of treatment with additional reinforcement to the membrane in those areas in accordance with the manufacturer's instructions. Blisters in asphalt coverings should be softened with a blow lamp and smoothed out. Badly cracked and crumbling asphalt should be completely removed and an asbestos underlay nailed or bonded to the roof in its place. Blisters in bitumen felt should be

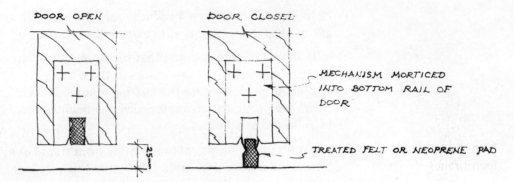

Figure 5/11 Automatic draught seal.

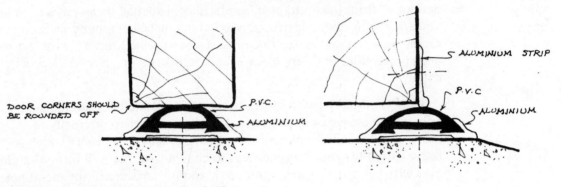

Figure 5/12 Aluminium/PVC spring threshold.

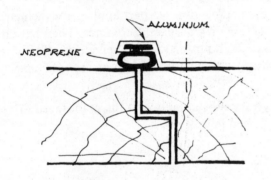

Figure 5/13 Compression device for meeting stiles (planted-on).

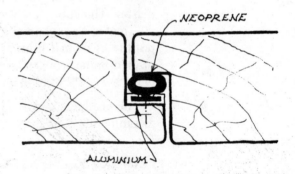

Figure 5/14 Compression device for meeting stiles (inset into rebate).

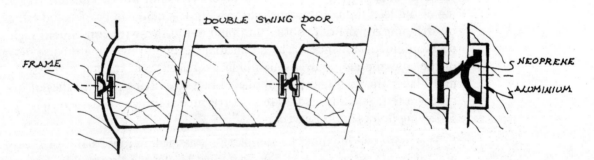

Figure 5/15 Wiping seals for double swing doors.

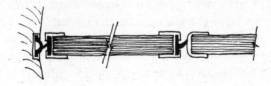

Figure 5/16 Wiping seals for armour plate glass doors.

cut, opened, cleaned and dried before being stuck down again with the treatment.

Treatments are tar/rubber based. On flat roofed areas they are made up of three layers of coating with a reinforcing membrane between the first and second layer. A blinding of 1.5 mm mineral chippings can be applied to the last layer.

On pitched roofs one manufacturer recommends a similar type of treatment and number of layers, while another is prepared to guarantee for five years a two layer application without reinforcing membrane.

The materials are usually black, but a coloured finish can be applied if desired. The products adhere well to various substrates and provide sufficient flexibility to overcome the normal movement in the roof structure. They can be used successfully on parapet and valley gutters and similar locations where old lead linings have cracked and are leaking. The treatment must, however, be carried far enough up under the slates or tiles to ensure freedom from leakage where the coating ends.

Finally it should be emphasised that it is important to establish the cause of the initial defect before applying one of the above treatments. If built-up felt roofing has split through excessive movement of the decking, or through inadequate and ineffective expansion joints, the imposition of a treatment such as those referred to above will prove only a temporary expedient. Such treatments do not have the degree of flexibility necessary to overcome major movement and the original splitting will eventually reappear.

The types of treatment detailed in this section are adequate only where the initial breakdown has not been brought about by mechanical distortion of the element concerned. In cases where distortion has occurred — and they may at times be difficult to recognise with certainty — elimination of the cause is the only effective action. This might well involve major reconstruction work, which is beyond the scope of this book.

SECONDARY ELEMENTS: DOORS AND WINDOWS

Failure of doors and windows to exlude air and water is usually associated with badly fitting opening sections. Leakage occurs between the opening unit and the surrounding frame. A difference between the air pressure on the outer face and that on the inner face of a door or window unit can cause rainwater to be retained in the gap — the long narrow slot — between the unit and its frame. The pumping action of a gusting wind may then drive this water inwards, in spite of throatings and drainage grooves in the rebate. All windows and doors will leak in certain conditions (See chapter 3). The aim is to ensure that they do not leak to any appreciable extent in the conditions which may reasonably be expected in the areas where they are used.

It is probably advantageous for opening lights of windows to allow the passage of a modest amount of air for reasons of ventilation. (Fully air conditioned buildings, of course, will not be provided with opening windows). This level of air leakage should be controlled and maintained within acceptable limits as explained in chapter 3. The devices discussed in this section are designed to control both air and water leakage and are produced either for insertion in existing installations, remedying an unsatisfactory condition, or for installation in the new element at the time of building. No distinction is made here between the two types of device,

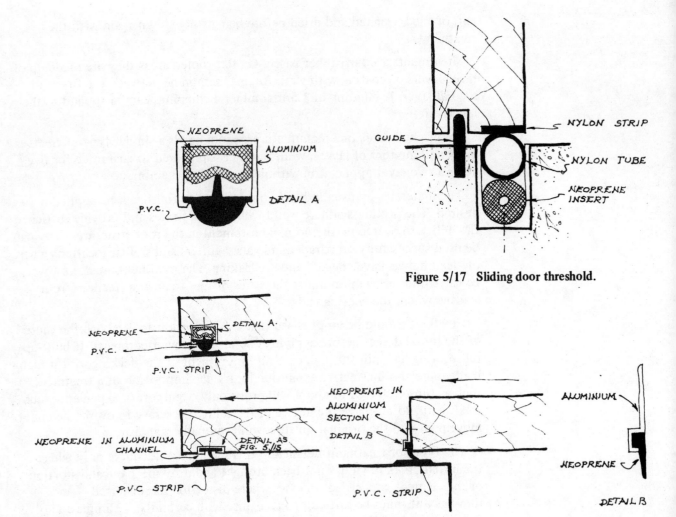

Figure 5/17 Sliding door threshold.

Figure 5/18 Sliding door jamb wiping seals.

although some are obviously easier to fix to an existing installation than others. Existing doors will usually have to be shot (planed) and re-hung, unless the device has in-built tolerances to overcome such variations in the gap size as have developed during the use of the door. Threshold seals are particularly difficult to fit to old doors, due to the tendency of the toe of the door to drop in use. For jambs and heads, seals compressing against the face of the door clearly provide a ready answer to the problem.

All other failures of secondary elements in this context can be associated with defective glazing putty, or sealant; and remedy is merely a matter of re-glazing, maybe with a more suitable sealant (see chapter 3).

Types of seal

There are four main types of seal:

a) compression seals (neoprene, rubber, plastics, foam and PVC)

b) spring strip (copper alloy, zinc, nylon)

c) wiping seal (neoprene, plastic)

d) brush weatherstrip (nylon, silicone impregnated wool or polypropylene)

The names are largely self-explanatory. Compression seals depend on the squeezing of a resilient material by the closing of a unit against its frame. This provides an air and weathertight seal. Spring strips are similarly deformed by

144

the closing of a hinged unit. The wiping seal depends on the friction of the seal against the opening section for its effectiveness. The brush weatherstrip is partially a compression strip, partially a wiping seal, depending on the hinged or sliding movement of the opening section.

Doors

Doors are usually less carefully detailed than windows, and one could expect them, therefore, to be less effective in keeping out water and draughts. This is not necessarily proved to be the case in practice — a fact that causes some bewilderment, but is probably connected with the ground level position of a door in the facade. This position at the foot of a wall may well obtain some local shelter provided by up-currents of the wind. There is still need for more research on this subject of the resistance of doors to air and water penetration.

Many of the details of weatherproofing devices are common to doors and windows. The hinged door is weathersealed at head and jambs by devices of a design which would also serve for casement windows. These are usually compression or spring strip seals, trapped in the rebate by the closing of the hinged section. One of the cheapest seals, though not very long-lasting, is the self-adhesive polyurethane or PVC foam strip (Figure 5/1). For a time the foam will retain its resilience and suffer no permanent deformation, but eventually it will lose its powers of recovery. A more sophisticated device is the aluminium/neoprene compression seal set into the rebate (Figure 5/2). This is likely to retain its resilience and effectiveness much longer. A planted-on version of this can be used round awkwardly shaped doors and windows (Figure 5/3). There are also several different types of metal spring strip devices (bronze, copper or zinc) for pinning into the rebates, which again depend on compression to function satisfactorily (Figure 5/4).

The detail at the foot of a door is a particularly difficult one, and one that is special to the door. The door face, being relatively non-absorbent, suffers a large build-up of water at its foot which has to be directed away from the interior. The traditional weatherboard and water bar was an unsophisticated way of dealing with the problem (Figure 5/5). Today there are various proprietary threshold devices available which overcome the ingress not only of water but also of draughts. A straightforward compression device developed from the water bar (Figure 5/6) can solve the problem as long as the door fits well against the device. Figure 5/7 illustrates one of several aluminium devices which collect the water which has run down the door and drain it away through weep holes. The weep holes must not be allowed to get blocked with dirt. An aluminium compression version of the traditional weatherboard (Figure 5/8) contains a neoprene tube which squeezes on to an aluminium threshold strip. Alternatively a similar neoprene tube in an aluminium channel can be let into the door step, or planted on top of the step (Figure 5/9). A two-part threshold (Figure 5/10) provides not only a compression seal, but a drained aluminium threshold as well.

All these devices aim to exclude both draughts and rain. There is also a range of bronze, felt or rubber draught exclusion devices which are fixed either to the inside face of the door or let into the underside of the door, and are raised automatically on the opening of the door (Figure 5/11). These are really effective only for draught exclusion and not for water exclusion. PVC spring threshold seals are sometimes used on external doors (Figure 5/12), but are more suited to internal doors.

The treatment of the meeting stiles of a double door is another detail

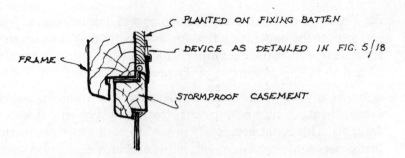

Figure 5/19 Wiping seals to top-hung window heads.

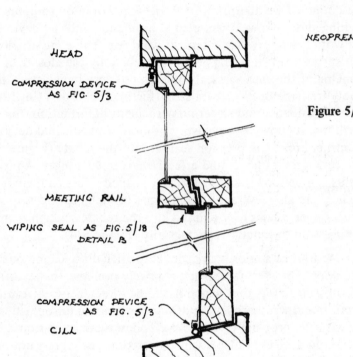

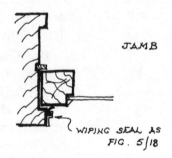

Figure 5/20 Wiping seals in bottom frame of casement.

Figure 5/21 Seals to double-hung sashes.

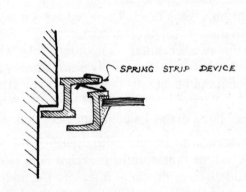

Figure 5/22 Metal window spring strip device.

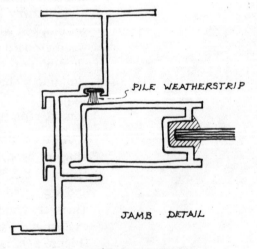

Figure 5/23 Pile weatherstrip for aluminium sliding window.

146

special to doors. Figure 5/13 shows a typical aluminium/neoprene compression device fixed on the opening side of the 'live' leaf of a pair of doors. A tidier handling of the detail is obtained by fixing a similar device in the rebate of the 'dead' leaf (Figure 5/14). In double swing doors the problem is greater. The threshold can be treated with an aluminium channel and neoprene tube threshold as above; the meeting stiles and the jambs, however, have to be dealt with by setting into the door leaves and the frames pairs of neoprene wiping seals and matching contact sections (Figure 5/15). This type of device is suitable for armourplate glass doors as well as timber doors (Figure 5/16).

The sliding door presents an even greater problem. The foot of the door can be weathersealed — not very successfully — by an inset device consisting of an aluminium channel and a nylon tube supported on a neoprene cushion. The nylon tube bears on the neoprene cushion, the latter carrying the weight of the door at all times (Figure 5/17). The jambs can be treated with a device combining a convex PVC contact section and a neoprene insert. This operates against a PVC or aluminium strip on each side of the opening (Figure 5/18).

Windows

Many of the compression and spring strip seals previously described for use at the jambs and heads of hinged doors are suitable also for timber casement windows. Neoprene wiping seals can be used externally to protect the head of top-hung, outward opening lights — a vulnerable joint in all so-called 'stormproof' standard timber windows (Figure 5/19). Similar inset neoprene wiping seals can be set into the bottom frame of timber outward opening lights, with compression seals in the jambs and head (Figure 5/20). Wiping and compression seals can also be used to weatherseal double-hung timber sashes (Figure 5/21), whilst standard metal windows can be fitted with metal spring strip devices that clip over the outer frame (Figure 5/22).

A specialist device which is frequently built-in at the manufacturing stage but only rarely applied as a remedial treatment is the pile weatherstrip. This is either nylon, silicone treated wool, or polypropylene pile, usually bonded to a thin aluminium strip for insertion into grooves in aluminium frame extrusions (Figure 5/23). Most sliding and double hung aluminium windows are provided with this type of device.

Factors to be considered

Correct fitting of a weatherseal is of paramount importance. If engagement with the device is not continuous and correctly adjusted, the desired result will not be achieved and damage can be caused — spring strips can be bent or torn off by the operation of incorrectly fitted doors; some neoprene inserts can be torn unless the doors compressing them have their leading edges rounded slightly; the edges of doors can be scratched or gouged by oversprung metal strips, and hinges can be subjected to strain by the use of an overlarge seal.

Another important fact which may be overlooked is that some seals are more noticeable than others. These are particularly vulnerable to damage from inquisitive or destructive individuals, and this should be borne in mind when selecting devices.

Appendix 1.
Glossary

absorbency	The capacity to take in liquid.
absorption	The act of taking in liquid.
adhesive seal	Seal made by the use of a non-setting compound, either gun or hand applied — often referred to as mastic seal.
air entraining agent	Chemical introduced into a concrete mix in order to disperse air bubbles in the mix.
ASTM	American Society for the Testing of Materials.
back-up material	Material used to fill a joint between components prior to the application of an adhesive seal. Material must be compatible with sealant and may be fibreboard, bitumen-free rope, expanded polystyrene etc.
baffle	Loose tongue inserted in an open drained joint, thus dividing the drainage area into two parts.
bead glazing	Glazing method in which a removable timber or metal strip is used to retain the bedded glass in position. Beads can be internal or external.
bed joints	Horizontal joints in brick, block, masonry or other mass walling.
BRE	Building Research Establishment of the Department of the Environment, based at Watford, England.
bridging	The action of moisture passing behind or around a damp proof membrane intended to prohibit its passage.
brush weather-strip	Weatherstripping, usually to window or door, using a strip of nylon or similar pile which is crushed by the closing of one frame or element against another.
BSI	British Standards Institution.
capillary channel	Fine hair crack along which water travels (against the force of gravity) due to surface tension.
catchment tray	*In open joint claddings*, horizontal trough in which water behind the cladding is collected prior to discharge outside the building.
	In tests of weathertightness, collection vessels at various points of the test specimen to measure water penetration.
CIB	Conseil Internationale du Bâtiment.

clearance	Minimum space permissible between two components to allow them to function, allowing for thermal and moisture movement and minimum joint size.
'cold-side'	In composite panels, the side outside the insulation, where interstitial condensation can become a danger.
component	A unit contributing to the construction of a whole building, e.g. wall panel.
compression seal	A seal that functions by being compressed between components in a dry joint and does not depend on adhesion with the components. A gasket.
cruciform gasket	A cross-shaped gasket which achieves its effect by the deformation of the arms of the cross in compression between components.
curtain wall	Wall made up of timber or steel framework into which are installed glazed or solid, opening or fixed panels.
direct glazing	Glazing to rebate in structure (usually concrete) without use of subsidiary frame.
distance pieces	Blocks placed in the glazing rebate between the rebate and the glass to prevent movement of the glass and displacement of the glazing compound under wind loading.
DOE	Department of the Environment.
double glazed unit	Glazing unit made up of two sheets of glass with a hermetically sealed vacuum between.
dpc	Damp proof course. An impermeable membrane to prevent the ingress of water into a building.
drainage area	In open drained joints, that part of the joint on the weather side of the components within which rain water drains away without reaching the air-tight seal at the rear.
drainage channels	Ways created within components to drain away moisture, whether from outside or due to condensation, without harm to the structure.
drained glazing	Glazing system that provides drainage channels within rebates to drain away harmlessly any water that penetrates the glazing compound — particularly used where glazing is by double glazed units.
drained joint	Open joint which relies on water entering the joint draining harmlessly away, due to the profile and design of the opposing faces of the joint, without reaching the air-tight seal at the rear of the joint.
driving-rain index	Index based on a combination of annual rainfall and average wind speed to give a measurement of exposure.

$$\frac{\text{Annual rainfall (mm) x average wind speed (M/S)}}{1000}$$
$$= \text{driving rain index in } m^2 / S$$

driving-rain roses	Diagrammatic method of relating both the amount of driving rain and its direction.
dry joint	A joint using a gasket and not relying on either a setting compound (mortar) or a non-setting sealant (mastic).
EFAB seal	Evacuated tube gasket designed in Sweden.
evacuated tube seal	Tube gasket from which the air is evacuated prior to placing, after which the vacuum is released to provide pressure to seal the joint.

150

face glazing	Method of glazing involving the use of putty instead of beads.
filled joint	A one stage joint made by either mortar, sealant or compressive gasket.
fir cone gasket	Triangular, ridged gasket of synthetic rubber or similar material used to form a seal between wall panel components.
fit	Reconciliation of requirements of joint clearance with performance requirements and unavoidable inaccuracies.
flashing	An impervious strip or sheet of material to prevent the penetration of water between the roof covering and an adjacent surface.
gasket	Compression seal which achieves its performance by its elasticity rather than by its adhesion to the adjacent components. Usually made of synthetic rubbers or thermoplastics.
grooved gasket	A form of structural glazing gasket, sometimes referred to as a 'Y' type gasket, with ridged spline for insertion in frame.
gun applied	Of mastics; applied by mechanical applicator as opposed to by hand.
'H' type gasket	A form of structural glazing gasket of an H shaped cross section.
heel bead	Strip of glazing sealant between the edge of the glass and the frame.
ICDG	Interdepartmental Construction Development Group of the Departments of Education & Science, Environment, Health and Social Security and the Scottish Development Department.
impermeable	Not permitting the passage of water or other liquid.
impervious	Not able to be penetrated; impermeable.
induced deviation	Man-made dimensional inaccuracies (usually of components) caused by manufacturing or other processes.
inherent deviation	Dimensional inaccuracies (usually of components) caused by the physical characteristics of the item, i.e. dimensional changes due to temperature or moisture fluctuations.
initial surface absorption	The amount of liquid absorbed by a unit area of component after a stated interval and at constant head and temperature.
interstitial condensation	The depositing of water vapour in the form of liquid within the thickness of a composite structure or panel, due to the air carrying the vapour reaching a surface whose temperature is lower than the dew point of the air.
inverted roof	A form of construction developed in Europe in which the insulation is placed above the weathering layer or membrane.
IRHD	International rubber hardness degree.
ISO	International Standards Organisation.
joint	The space between two adjacent components, irrespective of whether it is filled or not.
Knag gasket	A drained glazing gasket developed in Norway.
knife applied	Of mastic; applied by hand as opposed to by gun.
labyrinth joint	An open joint that depends on its profile to trap the water entering the joint and allow it to drain away before the joint is fully penetrated. It does not depend on an air seal at the rear of the joint.
ladder gasket	Structural glazing gasket of H, Y or single-sided types formed with factory-

moulded T junctions into multi-paned ladder-like assemblies, requiring no additional structural support within stated limits.

ledging position	Flat section of the structure which receives the load from a cladding unit.
loadbearing fixing	A fixing device that not only retains a unit (i.e. wall panel) in position, but also carries the weight (or part of the weight) of the unit.
loadbearing tape	Pre-formed strip of glazing compound. The word 'loadbearing' is not strictly correct, as tapes need not be totally loadbearing. Only a pre-shimmed tape is fully loadbearing.
location blocks	Blocks of resilient, non-absorbent material placed in the glazing rebate at jambs and head to ensure that the glass is central in the frame and that edge clearances are maintained.
mastic	Non-setting adhesive sealant.
moisture movement	Reversible dimensional change produced by a component absorbing or losing water.
movement joint	A joint designed to accept movement in the structure or claddings without impairing its weather sealing properties.
NAAM	National Association of Architectural Metal Manufacturers.
non-reversible movement	Movement of structure or component due to the physical characteristics of its composition and leading to a one-way dimensional change, e.g. shrinkage of concrete frame or component.
one-part sealant	A sealing compound not requiring the addition of a curing agent.
one-stage joint	A joint, such as a filled joint, that relies on only one defense against the ingress of water.
permeable	Allowing the passage of liquids.
permissible manufacturing deviation	Maximum amount of dimensional tolerance (plus or minus) acceptable in a component without contravening the requirements of fit.
perpend	Vertical joint in brickwork.
pervious	Allowing penetration by liquid.
porous	Containing minute pores or interstices which allow penetration by liquid.
preformed tape	sealant in the form of a strip for simple economic application.
pre-shimmed tape	Loadbearing glazing compound in strip form, including a rod of synthetic rubber to act as a distance piece.
rain-screen cladding	Open joint cladding designed to provide substantial protection to the wall structure behind by encouraging the rain water to drain away in the ventilated cavity behind the cladding.
restraint fixing	A fixing designed to retain a component in position but not to carry its weight.
reveal	The vertical side of an opening in a wall between any frame built in the opening and the face of the wall.
reversible movement	Movement of structure or component due to its reaction to changes in temperature or moisture level.
sarking felt	Bitumen felt covering over pitched roof spars before the fixing of tile or slate battens.
seal	Device or composition to prevent air and/or water penetration of a joint.

sealant	Composition applied to a joint by hand, gun, knife or trowel, by pouring or in strip form with the intention of creating a seal between adjacent units and maintaining this despite movement in the joint.
setting blocks	Blocks of resilient, non-absorbent material placed in the glazing rebate at a cill to ensure that the glass is central in the frame and that edge clearances are maintained.
shell bedding	Method of laying concrete blocks in which a solid bed of mortar is not used, but merely a strip of mortar along front and back edges of the blocks.
shield	In open joint cladding, an impervious strip behind the joint to ensure harmless drainage of the rainwater penetrating the joint.
shrinkage	A non-reversible movement of a structure or component as occurs, for example, in the ageing of concrete.
side flow	The sideways flow of rainwater from the front face of components into the vertical joints between those components.
single-sided gasket	A form of structural glazing gasket which differs from the 'H' and 'Y' types in that the glass is not retained between the arms of the gasket, but is retained from one side by the gasket pressing the glass against a rebate.
slip cill	A non-stooled cill; i.e. one that does not have squared ends for building into the wall at each side of the opening.
spring strip	A form of metal weather stripping to doors or opening lights of windows.
soakers	Pieces of flexible metal fitted to interlock with slates or tiles to make a watertight joint between wall and roof, or at a hip or valley.
solid bedded glazing	A form of bead glazing in which the glass is set in the rebate solidly in glazing compounds or sealants.
stooling	The squared end of an inclined weathered cill for building in to the walling.
structural gasket	Glazing gasket of the 'H', 'Y' or single sided type made of synthetic rubber or similar material.
thermal movement	Reversible dimensional change produced in a component or structure by its reaction to temperature changes.
through-fixing	The fixing achieved when a fixing device passes through the component to be fixed.
transferred function	A function of a wall panel which needs to be reproduced in the character of the joint in order to produce continuity of performance.
two-part sealant	A sealant requiring the addition of a curing agent to the compound before application.
two-stage joint	A joint which does not rely on only a single method of weather protection, e.g. a drained joint.
vapour barrier	An impervious membrane to prohibit the passage of internal humid air into structural cavities in which condensation could occur.
vision strip	In bead glazing, a strip pushed into the heel bead between the glass and the glazing bead to act as a continuous distance piece and produce compression between glass and sealant.
'washboard' grooves	Grooves in the opposing faces of a drained joint which encourage water entering the joint to drain away from the interior of the joint.
water check grooves	Grooves that discourage the flow of water through moveable joints.

weather bar	A rigid metal strip at the foot of a door or window to prevent the flow of water inwards.
weather stripping	A rain or wind exclusion device for use in the rebates of opening lights of windows or doors.
wiping seal	A seal that achieves its effect by distortion due to the rubbing of the seal against a frame or other component.
'Y' type gasket	A form of structural glazing gasket of a Y shaped cross section.
zipper strip	A locking strip of tough synthetic rubber inserted into cavities in structural glazing gaskets of Y or H types after the positioning of the glass, thereby exerting compressive forces on the glass.

Appendix 2.
Schedule of Advisory Bodies

Agrément Board,
Lord Alexander House,
Waterhouse Street,
Hemel Hempstead, Herts.
HP1 1DH.

Aluminium Federation,
Broadway House, Calthorpe Road,
Five Ways, Birmingham B15 1TN.

Asbestos Cement Manufacturers Association,
15 Tooks Court,
London EC4A 1LA.

Brick Development Association (BDA)
19 Grafton Street,
London W1X 3LE.

British Plastics Federation,
47 Piccadilly,
London W1V 0DN.

British Standards Institution,
British Standards House,
2 Park Street, London W1A 2BS.

British Steel Corporation,
Steel Sheet Information Centre, P O Box 142,
151 Gower Street,
London WC1E 6BB.

Building Research Establishment

   Building Research Station,
   Garston, Watford WD2 7JR.

   Princes Risborough Laboratory,
   Princes Risborough,
   Aylesbury, Buckinghamshire HP17 9PX.

   Building Research Establishment
      Scottish Laboratory,
   Kelvin Road, East Kilbride,
   Glasgow G75 0RZ.

Cement and Concrete Association,
52 Grosvenor Gardens,
London SW1 W0AQ.

Copper Development Association,
Orchard House,
Mutton Lane,
Potters Bar, Hertfordshire EN6 3AP.

Felt Roofing Contractors Advisory Board,
Maxwelton House,
Boltro Road, Haywards Heath,
West Sussex RH16 1BJ.

Insulation Glazing Association,
6 Mount Row,
London W1Y 6DY.

Lead Development Association,
Technical Information Bureau,
34 Berkeley Square,
London W1X 6AJ.

Light Facades Development Council,
11 Sandhurst Close,
South Croydon, Surrey CR2 0AD.

Patent Glazing Conference,
13 Upper High Street,
Epsom, Surrey KT17 4QY.

Rubber and Plastics Research Association of Great Britain,
Shawbury, Shrewsbury, Shropshire.

Sandlime Brick Manufacturers Association (SBMA).
Lloyds Bank Chambers,
3 Town Square, Stevenage SG1 1BP.

Sealant Manufacturers' Conference (SMC),
15 Tooks Court,
London EC4A 1LA.

Zinc Development Association,
34 Berkeley Square,
London W1X 6AJ.

U.S.A.

American Society for Testing and Materials,
1916 Race Street,
Philadelphia PA 19103.

International Conference of Building Officials,
Whittier,
California.

Appendix 3.
Schedule of relevant
Codes of Practice
and Standards

BS Codes of Practice

CP 121	Code of Practice for Walling
Part 1:1973	Brick and block masonry
CP 142	Slating and tiling
Part 2:1971	Metric units
CP 143	Sheet roof and wall coverings
Part 1:1958	Aluminium, Corrugated and Troughed
Part 5:1964	Zinc
Part 6:1962	Corrugated asbestos cement
Part 10:1973	Galvanized corrugated steel
Part 11:1970	Lead
Part 12:1970	Copper
Part 15:1973	Aluminium
Part 16:1974	Semi-rigid asbestos bitumen sheet
CP 144	Roof coverings
Part 3:1970	Built-up bitumen felt
Part 4:1970	Mastic asphalt
CP 145	Glazing systems
Part 1:1969	Patent glazing
CP 151	Doors and windows including frames and linings
Part 1:1957	Wooden doors
CP 152:1972	Glazing and fixing of glass for buildings
CP 153	Windows and rooflights
Part 1:1969	Cleaning and safety
Part 2:1970	Durability and maintenance
CP 297:1972	Precast concrete cladding (non-loadbearing)
CP 298:1972	Natural stone cladding (non-loadbearing)
CP 308:1974	Drainage of roofs and paved areas

British Standards

BS 187	Calcium silicate (sandlime and flintlime) bricks
Part 2:1970	Metric units

BS 402 Part 2:1970	Clay plain roofing tiles and fittings Metric units
BS 473 & 550 Part 2:1971	Concrete roofing tiles and fittings Metric units
BS 476 Part 3:1975	Fire tests on building materials and structures External fire exposure roof test

BS 644
    Part 1:1951
    Part 2:1958
    Part 3:1951
	Wood windows
	Wood casement windows
	Wood double hung sash windows
	Wood double hung sash and case windows (Scottish type)

BS 680 Part 2:1971	Roofing slates Metric units

BS 690
    Part 1:1963
    Part 2:1971
    Part 3:1973
    Part 4:1974
    Part 5:1975
    Part 6:1976
	Asbestos-cement slates and sheets
	Asbestos-cement slates, corrugated sheets and semi-compressed flat sheets
	Flat sheets, semi and fully compressed
	Corrugated sheets
	Slates
	Lining sheets and panels
	Fittings for use with corrugated sheets

BS 747 Part 2:1970	Roofing felts Metric units
BS 849:1939	Plain sheet zinc roofing

BS 903
    Part A2:1971
    Part A6:1969
    Part A19:1956
    Part A23:1963
    Part A25:1968
    Part A26:1969
	Methods of testing vulcanized rubber
	Determination of tensile stress-strain properties
	Determination of compression set after constant strain
	Accelerated ageing tests
	Determination of resistance to ozone cracking under static conditions
	Determination of impact brittleness temperature
	Determination of hardness

BS 988, 1076, 1097, 1451:1973	Mastic asphalt for building (limestone aggregate)
BS 990 Part 2: 1972	Steel windows generally for domestic and similar buildings Metric units
BS 1178:1969	Milled lead sheet and strip for building purposes
BS 1180:1972	Concrete bricks and fixing bricks
BS 1217:1975	Cast stone
BS 1470:1972	Wrought aluminium and aluminium alloys for general engineering purposes — plate, sheet and strip
BS 1787:1951	Steel windows for industrial buildings
BS 1881 Part 5:1970	Methods of testing concrete Methods of testing hardened concrete for other than strength
BS 2028, 1364:1968	Precast concrete blocks
BS 2870:1968	Rolled copper and copper alloys. Sheet, strip and foil
BS 3083:1959	Hot-dipped galvanized corrugated steel sheets for general purposes
BS 3712 Part 1:1974	Methods of test for building sealants Homogeneity, specific gravity, extrudability, penetration and slump

Part 2:1973	Seepage, staining, shrinkage, alkali resistance, shelf life and paintability
Part 3:1974	Application time, change in consistency, skinning properties, tack-free time and adhesion of fresh material to mature sealant
BS 3826:1969	Silicone-based water repellents for masonry
BS 3921:1974	Clay bricks and blocks
BS 4036:1966	Asbestos-cement fully compressed flat sheets
BS 4154:1967	Corrugated plastics translucent sheets made from thermosetting polyester resins (glass fibre reinforced)
BS 4254:1967	Two-part polysulphide-based sealants for the building industry
BS 4255	Preformed rubber gaskets for weather exclusion from buildings
Part 1:1967	Non-cellular gaskets
Part 2:1975	Cellular gaskets
BS 4315	Methods of test for resistance to air and water penetration
Part 1:1968	Windows and gasket-glazing systems
Part 2:1970	Permeable walling constructions (water penetration)
BS 4476:1969	Asbestos-cement siding shingles
BS 4868:1972	Profiled aluminium sheet for building
BS 4873:1972	Aluminium alloy windows
BS 5390:1976	Code of Practice for Stone Masonry (Formerly CP 121:201 and CP 121:202)

Drafts for Development

DD4:1971	Recommendations for the grading of windows. Resistance to wind loads, air infiltration and water penetration and notes on window security.
DD22:1972	Recommendations for the co-ordination of dimensions in building. Tolerances and fits for building. The calculation of work sizes and joint clearances for building components.

International Standards

ISO R37:1968	Determination of tensile stress-strain properties of vulcanized rubbers. (Agrees with BS 903 Part A2)
ISO R48:1968	Determination of hardness of vulcanized rubbers. (Agrees with relevant part of BS 903 Part A26)
ISO R188:1961	Accelerated ageing or simulated service tests of vulcanized natural or synthetic rubbers. (Agrees with BS 903 Part A19)
ISO R393:1964	Asbestos-cement corrugated sheets for roofing and cladding. (BS 690 Part 3:1973 implements)
ISO R394:1964	Asymmetrical-section corrugated sheets in asbestos-cement for roofing and cladding. (BS 690 Part 3:1973 implements)
ISO R395:1964	Asbestos-cement slates for roofing and cladding. (substantially agrees with BS 690 Part 4:1974)
ISO R396:1964	Asbestos-cement flat sheets. (substantially agrees with BS 690 Part 2:1971)
ISO R880:1968	Asbestos-cement siding shingles. (in technical agreement with BS 4476 1969)

U.S.A. Standards

Relevant Uniform Building Code Standards   (International Conference of Building Officials, Whittier, California.)

Standards applicable to Uniform Building Code, Section 2403, Chapter 24, Masonry.

UBCS 24 – 1	Building brick, facing brick and hollow brick (made from clay or shale) based on ASTM specifications C 62 – 58, C 216 – 66 and C 652 – 70
UBCS 24 – 2	Sand-lime building brick based on ASTM specification C 73 – 67
UBCS 24 – 3	Concrete building brick based on ASTM specification C 55 – 55
UBCS 24 – 4	Hollow load-bearing concrete masonry units based on ASTM specification C 90 – 70
UBCS 24 – 5	Solid load-bearing concrete masonry units based on ASTM specification C 145 – 59
UBCS 24 – 6	Hollow non-load-bearing concrete masonry units based on ASTM specification C 129 – 59
UBCS 24 – 7	Method of test for concrete masonry units based on ASTM specification C 140 – 70
UBCS 24 – 8	Structural clay load-bearing wall tile and standard methods of sampling and testing structural clay tile based on ASTM specifications C 34 – 70 and C 112 – 70
UBCS 24 – 14	Cast stone based on the specification AC1. 704-44 of American Concrete Institute.
UBCS 24 – 17	Cement, masonry based on ASTM specification C 91 – 67
UBCS 24 – 18	Quicklime for structural purposes based on ASTM specification C 5 – 59
UBCS 24 – 19	Hydrated lime for masonry purposes based on ASTM specification C 207 – 49
UBCS 24 – 20	Processed pulverized quicklime based on ASTM specification C 51 – 47
UBCS 24 – 21	Mortar for unit masonry and reinforced masonry other than gypsum based on ASTM specification C 161 – 44T and C 270 – 59T
UBCS 24 – 22	Aggregate for masonry mortar based on ASTM specification C 144 – 70

Standards applicable to Uniform Building Code, Section 2603, Chapter 26, Concrete.

UBCS 26 – 10	Concrete tests based on ASTM specifications C 31 – 69, C 39 – 71, C 42 – 68, C 78 – 64, C 192 – 69 and C 617 – 71

Standards applicable to Uniform Building Code, Section 3203, Chapter 32, Roof construction and covering.

UBCS 32 – 1	Materials for use in construction of built-up roof coverings based on standard specification 55–A (1968) of the Underwriters' Laboratories, Inc.

UBCS 32 – 2	Roofing asphalt based on ASTM specification D 312 – 44
UBCS 32 – 3	Composition roofing based on standard specification 55–B (1962) of the Underwriters' Laboratories, Inc.
UBCS 32 – 4	Sheet metals based on ASTM specifications A 245 – 62 aT, A 361 – 63T and B 209 – 62
UBCS 32 – 5	Roofing aggregates based on recommended standards of the International Conference of Building Officials.
UBCS 32 – 9	Asbestos - cement shingles based on ASTM specification C 222 – 60
UBCS 32 – 10	Slate shingles based on ASTM specification C 406 – 57 T
UBCS 32 – 12	Roofing tiles based on recommended standards of the International Conference of Building Officials

Standards applicable to Uniform Building Code, Section 5401, Chapter 54, Glass and glazing.

UBCS 54 – 1	Glass based on Federal Specification DD-G-00451C U.S. Federal Government.

Additional ASTM specifications (American Society for Testing and Materials, Philadelphia)

ASTM C542 – 71A	Lock-strip gaskets
ASTM E283 – 73	Rate of air leakage through exterior windows, curtain walls and doors.
ASTM E330 – 70	Structural performance of exterior windows, curtain walls and doors under the influence of wind loads.
ASTM E331 – 70	Water penetration of exterior windows, curtain walls and doors by uniform static pressure differential

ASTM tests for properties required of a sealant: –

D395	compression
D412	tensile
D570	water absorption
D676	hardness
D746	low temperature brittleness
D865	heat ageing
D1149	ozone resistance

Other U.S.A. standards

Federal Specifications

TT – C – 598	Compound calking: plastic (for masonry and other structures)
TT – S – 00227a	Sealing compound; rubber base, two component (for calking, sealing and glazing in building construction)

National Association of Architectural Metal Manufacturers standard

NAAM Standard TM – 1 – 68T Method of test for metal curtain walls

American National Standards Institute specifications

ANSI A134.1 – 1972   Specification for aluminium windows

ANSI A134.2 – 1972   Specification for aluminium sliding glass doors

Aluminium Window Manufacturers Association specification

AWMA Bulletin 100.
1959   Specification performance test program and procedures.

Appendix 4.
Bibliography

Agrément Board MOAT No. 1 Windows 1967
MOAT No. 7 Doors
Information Sheet No. 1 – Windows

Architects Journal Handbook. Doors. Technical Study 5: Sealing and
perforations.

Architects Journal Technical Study – The inverted roof. 14th May, 1975

ASTM Special Publication 552, Window and Wall testing. 1972

Building Research Establishment Advisory Service
Leaflet TIL 41 Amended 1974. Insulating cavity fills
for dwellings.

Building Research Station Current Papers

CP 29/70   Harrison, H.W., Bonshor, R.B.,
Weatherproofing of joints: a systematic approach to
design. 1970.

CP 33/71   Skeen, J.W., Experiments on the rain penetration of
brickwork: the effect of mortar type. 1971

CP 10/73   Herbert, M.R.M, Cronshaw, J.L.,
Width variations of cladding joints. 1973

CP 56/74   Cronshaw, J.L., Study of drained glazing techniques for
factory made hermetically sealed double glazing window
units. Final report. 1974.

CP 81/74   Herbert, M.R.M., Some observations on the behaviour of
weather protective features on external walls. 1974.

CP 86/74   Herbert, M.R.M., Window to wall joints. 1974.

CP 89/74   Herbert, M.R.M., Open-jointed rain screen claddings. 1974.

CP 90/74   Herbert, M.R.M., Harrison, H.W., New ways with weatherproof joints. 1974.

Building Research Station Digests. HMSO

45 and 46   Design and appearance – Parts 1 and 2.

85   Joints between concrete wall panels: open drained joints.
1967, revised 1971.

119   Assessment of wind loads. 1974.

Building Research Station Digests (cont)

126	Changes in the appearance of concrete on exposure. 1971.
127	An index of exposure to driving rain. 1971.
137	Principles of joint design. 1972.
144	Asphalt and built-up felt roofings: durability. 1972.
160	Mortars for bricklaying.

Building Research Establishment — Princes Risborough Laboratory.

Skinner, N.P. Performance of building components. 1975

Felt Roofing Contractors Advisory Board
Built-up roofing.

Gage, Michael, and Kirkbride, T.,
Design in Blockwork. Architectural Press,
and Cement and Concrete Association. 1972.

Insulation Glazing Association. IGA glazing requirements and procedures for gasket glazing of double windows and hermetically sealed double glazing units (insulating glass).

Interdepartmental Construction Development Group.
Technical Note No. 1 Performance requirements for windows.

Lewis, Roger J.   Come wind, come rain. The Architect. April 1973.

Light Facades Development Council. Design aspects of joints in light facades (excluding glazing joints) Bulletin 4. 1971.

Marsh, Paul.   Concrete as a visual material. Cement and Concrete Association. 1974.

NFBTE, BRE, Agrément Board, NHBC. Guide to the use of urea formaldehyde foam cavity insulation in new construction.

Norwegian Building Research Institute.

Paper 0-2801   Window test method

Report E 4023 Driving rain and ventilated sheathings with open joints.

Report 51C   Recent Canadian experience in wall design.

CIB Report 11 Bishop, D., The performance of drained joints. 1968.

Sealant Manufacturers Conference Reports

SMC 5   One-part gun-grade polysulphide sealants for the construction industry. 1970.

SMC 10   One-part silicon based sealants for glazing applications and sanitary ware in the construction industry. 1972.

Taylor, K.H.   Jointing in cladding. Rubber and Plastics Research Association.

Appendix 5.
Characteristics of Some Proprietary Sealants

Types

A = acrylic
B = butyl
B/O = synthetic rubber/processed oils
Bit = bitumen

E = epoxy
E/P = epoxy/polysulphide
O = oil based
P(1) = one part polysulphide

P(2) = two part polysulphide
Polyu = polyurethane
Polyu/E = polyurethane/epoxy
Polyt = polythene

Pb = Polyisobutylene
R/Bit = rubber/bitumen
S = silicone

Application

G = gun applied
K = knife applied
Pr = poured
T = tape

Name	Type	Application	Standards applicable	Uses				% movement	Joint sizes		Temperature range °C	Life (years)	Comments
				Glazing	Construction joints	Minor joints and pointing	Expansion joints		Width (mm)	Depth (mm)			
Adshead Ratcliffe & Co. Ltd													
Arbosil 1081	S	G	SMC 10	X	X	X	—	25	3–35	3–12	-60 to +200	25	
Arbomast G.P.	O	G	—	—	—	X	—	10–25	5–25	6–18	-10 to +70	10	
Arbocrylic	A	G	—	X	X	X	—	20	5–18	6–18	-40 to +90	15–20	
Arbokol 1000	P(1)	G	SMC 5	X	X	X	—	25	5–25	6–15	-40 to +90	25	
Arbokol 2000	P(2)	G	BS 4254	X	X	—	X	35	min. 5	6–25	-50 to +100	25	Arbokol 2150 similar except not to BS 4254 and with only 20% movement

Adshead Ratcliffe & Co. Ltd (cont)

Name	Type	Application	Standards applicable	Uses: Glazing	Construction joints	Minor joints and pointing	Expansion joints	% movement	Width (mm)	Depth (mm)	Temperature range °C	Life (years)	Comments
Arbokol Plastomer	P(2)	K + G	—	X	—	X	—	10	5–15	6–12	-57 to +100	25	Glass jointing
Arboseal Butyl 88, P1B & 907	B	T	—	—	—	X	—	2–5	—	—	-40 to +100	—	Translucent sheeting sealing
Arboseal 03–SV and BR	Polyt or B	T	—	—	—	X	—	2–5	—	—	-30 to +90	—	Asbestos sheeting sealing
Arboseal LB and 06/11	—	T	—	X	—	X	—	2–5	—	—	-30 to +200	—	
Arboseal MS	—	T	—	X	—	—	—	2–5	—	—	-20 to +200	—	Internal glazing
Arbo Putty	O	K	—	X	—	—	—	—	—	—	—	—	Softwood frames free glazing
Arbolite	O	K	—	X	—	—	—	—	—	—	—	—	Metal frames face glazing
Arboflex	—	K	—	X	—	—	—	—	—	—	—	—	Bead glazing compound
Arbomast 500BR + BR	—	—	—	X	—	—	—	—	—	—	—	—	Edge filling and capping in moderate exposures
Arbo 2 Part glazing compound	B(2)	—	—	X	—	—	—	—	—	—	—	—	Ditto in severe exposures

Expandite Limited

Name	Type	Application	Standards applicable	Uses: Glazing	Construction joints	Minor joints and pointing	Expansion joints	% movement	Width (mm)	Depth (mm)	Temperature range °C	Life (years)	Comments
Thioflex-one	P(1)	G	SMC 5	—	X	X	—	10–20	3–20	6–20	-30 to +70	25	
Thioflex 600	P(2)	G or P_r	BS 4254 ASA.A116.1 US Fed. TT–S–227 a & b	—	X	—	X	25	3–40	6–25	-40 to +100	25	

Expandite Limited (cont.)

Name	Type	Application	Standards applicable	Glazing	Construction joints	Minor joints and pointing	Expansion joints	% movement	Width (mm)	Depth (mm)	Temperature range °C	Life (years)	Comments
High duty	P(2)	P_r	SS–S170	–	X	–	X	25	10–63	13–50	-40 to +60	10	
Silicone sealant	S	G	SMC 10	X	–	X	X	20	3–25	5–20	-40 to +121	25	Underwater application
Secoflex	B	G	–	–	X	X	X	25	6–35	13–25	-40 to +80	15	
Secomastic/Seelastik	B/O	G or K	–	–	–	–	X	–	5–25	10–62	-40 to +50	15	
Plastiseal	R/Bit	G or K	–	–	X	–	X	15–25	10–62	13–40	-18 to +82	10	
Seelastrip	B/O	P_r	–	X	X	–	–	–	–	–	-18 to +100	50	
Sealband	Polyu	T	–	–	X	X	–	–	–	–	-50 to +80	50	
Pliastic (various grades)	R/Bit	P_r	BS 2499 US Fed. SS.S.164	–	–	–	X	10–25	15–63	25–50	-15 to +50	5	Roads and runways
Aerolastic	R/Bit	P_r	BS 2499 SS.S.167b	–	–	–	X	10–25	15–63	25–50	-15 to +50	5	Roads and runways
Plastijoint	Bit	K	–	–	X	–	X	10	19–38	13–35	-10 to +80	10	In construction where appearance not important
Asbestumen	Bit	G + K	–	–	X	X	–	5	5–25	12–25	0 to +50	10	Asbestos sheeting etc.
Safeseal (various grades)	B/O	–	–	X	–	–	–	–	–	–	–	–	

Name	Type	Application	Standards applicable	Glazing	Construction joints	Minor joints and pointing	Expansion joints	% movement	Width (mm)	Depth (mm)	Temperature range °C	Life (years)	Comments
Kelseal Limited													
Kelseal P/R	P(2)	G	BS 4254 ASA.A166.1	X	X	—	X	30	—	not less than 6.35mm not to exceed ½ joint width	-40 to +100		
Glasticon 235/237	O	G	—	—	—	X	—	7.5	12 max.	6 min.	-30 to +80	2–5	
Glasticon 238	B	G	—	—	—	X	—	12.5	12 max.	6 min.	-30 to +100	10–20	
Kelbond ADN	N	G	—	—	—	X	—	—	—	—	-25 to +50	10–20	
Kelseal EPSA	E/P(2)	G	—	X	—	—	—	—	—	—	—	—	Double glazed units and armour clad glass doors
Glasticord 305	B/O	T	—	—	—	X	—	—	—	—	-30 to +175	—	Corrugated sheets
Glasticord 400	B	T	—	X	—	X	—	5	—	—	-30 to +180	10–20	
Glasticord 440	B	T	—	—	X	X	—	5	—	—	-40 to +150	10–20	
Glasticord 450	Poly-mer oils	T	—	X	—	X	—	—	—	—	-30 to +180	—	
Glasticord 935	B/O	T	—	—	—	X	—	—	—	—	min. -30	—	

Name	Type	Application	Standards applicable	Uses				% movement	Joint sizes		Temperature range °C	Life (years)	Comments
				Glazing	Construction joints	Minor joints and pointing	Expansion joints		Width (mm)	Depth (mm)			
Kelseal Limited (cont.)													
Glasticon—general purpose mastic	B/O	G	—	—	—	X	—	7.5	5–25	5–25	-30 to +70	—	
Glasticon 303	O	K	—	X	—	—	—	—	—	—	-20 to +200	—	Putty
Glasticon 480	B	K	—	X	—	X	—	—	—	—	-40 to +200	—	
Glasticon 16.279	B/O	G	—	X	—	—	—	—	—	—	-20 to +180	—	Bedding double glazed units
Tremco Limited													
Mono-lasto-meric	A	G	TTS 00230	—	X	X	X	33	6–25	6–12	-35 to +92	20+	
Dymeric	Polyu/ E(2)	G	TTS 00227E	—	X	X	X	50	6–50	6–25	-35 to +92	20	
Lasto-meric	P(2)	G	BS4254	X	X	X	X	25	6–25	6–12	-40 to +125	20	
Durabilt	O	G	—	—	X	X	—	10	6–19	6–19	-35 to +92	10	
PIB	Pb	G	—	X	—	X	—	—	—	—	-40 to +90	15	
Tremfill interior caulk	A	G	—	—	—	X	—	15	6–25	6–25	-35 to +92	15	
Pre-shimmed tape	Pb	T	—	X	—	—	—	—	—	—	-40 to +93	20	
440 tape	Pb	T	—	X	—	X	—	—	—	—	-40 to +93	20	
Small joint sealant·	A	G	—	—	—	small	—	10	3 max.	3 max.	—	10	

Index